Roland Schrapp

nt and Modern World View
ner's Criticism of Astrology

Titelbild:
Part of an illustration from Hartmann Schedel's "World Chronicle" on the spheres of our solar system (1493)

Roland Schrapp

Ancient and Modern World View

Rudolf Steiner's Criticism of Astrology

English edition of the German book "Das alte und das neue Weltbild – Rudolf Steiners Kritik der Astrologie"

Bibliographical information of the German National Library:
The German National Library lists this publication in the German National Bibliography. Detailed bibliographic data are available on the Internet at www.dnb.de.

© 2024 Roland Schrapp

Production and Publishing: BoD – Books on Demand, Norderstedt (Germany)

ISBN: 9783759742827

Contents

Introduction	7
Rudolf Steiner's opinion on astrology	11
The gradual decline of knowledge of the zodiac	24
The clairvoyant vision of the extrasensory zodiacal images	24
The determination of individual stars as physically visible markers between the zodiacal images	40
The definition of twelve constellations to replace the spatial areas of the fading zodiacal images	42
The non-consideration of the precession of the vernal equinox in Greek astrology	47
The projection of the zodiac into the depths of space	55
Synopsis of the ancient world view with today's world view	60
The lost knowledge of the house system	68
The importance of the point of sunrise for the development of mankind	70
The importance of the point of sunrise for the house system	74
The future turn of science towards the forces of the cosmos	78
The date of the laying of the foundation stone for the first Goetheanum	83
Epilog	89
List of Figures	93

Introduction

In Rudolf Steiner's anthroposophy, the zodiac and the planets are of great importance. The human being is characterized as a microcosm that is modelled on the macrocosm. In several lectures, Rudolf Steiner explains the hidden connection between the twelve zodiacal images and the human form[1] as well as the relationship between individual human organs and the planets of our solar system [2].

Furthermore, Rudolf Steiner describes in great detail the development of the soul-spiritual human being after death, his ascent into "planetary spheres" and even higher spheres, in which important phases of development and maturity are passed through. From there, the human being usually descends again into a new life on earth only after many centuries.[3] The term "planetary spheres" does not, of course, refer to the physical planets, but to extrasensory planes of existence whose center is the earth and whose boundaries roughly correspond to the orbits of the physical planets.

The early cosmological world views of mankind were based on these "spheres". The planets in the night sky and also the sun were primarily seen as physically visible representatives of different planes of existence, in which beings live and work that were only accessible to ancient clairvoyance, and which, in their various stages of development, far surpass humanity.

---

[1] e.g. GA 208 "Anthroposophie als Kosmosophie – Zweiter Teil" (Anthroposophy as Cosmosophy – Part 2), Dornach, 1921, 11 lectures

[2] e.g. GA 128 "Eine okkulte Physiologie" (An Occult Physiology), Prague, 1911, 8 lectures

[3] e.g. GA 140 "Okkulte Untersuchungen über das Leben zwischen Tod und neuer Geburt" (Investigations Into Life Between Death and Rebirth), various cities, 1912/1913, 20 lectures

Today, many people are concerned with the question of whether extraterrestrial life exists, perhaps even intelligent life? Asking such a question would never have occurred to people in the millennia before the birth of Christ. It would have seemed quite absurd to them, because due to their innate ability of extrasensory perception, which was carefully cultivated and encouraged in mystery schools, they often experienced the presence of higher beings with whom they could communicate and whom they could ask for advice on the concerns and needs of their nation. People of that time experienced our entire solar system as inhabited by entities that were not perceptible to physical eyes.

Since the old clairvoyance has faded and humanity's ability of perception has been completely limited to the physical sensory world, the planetary region around us seems to be empty and barren. Many of us today feel lonely in the cosmos, especially the inhabitants of Western civilization. Astronomers make considerable efforts to search for material traces of extraterrestrial life or even extra-terrestrial civilizations. However, these are imagined to consist of coarse matter. The focus on physical matter has become so massive that any thought of supernatural and therefore extrasensory levels of existence seems completely unrealistic to many people.

Things were quite different in past eras. Until the Age of Enlightenment and the beginning of the epoch of modern natural science, the vast majority of people were still completely convinced of the existence of higher beings living on higher planes. Only a few centuries ago, when the materialistic world view came to the fore, people began to smile at the ancient teachings of the planetary spheres, of the zodiac and the house system, and no longer took them seriously. This was partly justified, as the original knowledge has increasingly fallen into decay in the course of human development. The more the ancient clairvoyance faded, the more fantasy and superstition, on the one hand, and purely abstract considerations and conclusions, on the other, were mixed in, which led to many misinterpretations of the knowledge of the ancient cultures.

This book deals with this historical process. With the help of Rudolf Steiner's statements, the reader gains access to the original knowledge of the zodiac and the house system, both of which can only be found in today's astrology in a very disfigured and therefore sometimes completely distorted way.

In addition, the inner connection between the world view of the ancient cultures and our modern world view is explained.

Rudolf Steiner's opinion on astrology

A central component of Rudolf Steiner's teachings is the concept of the human being as a microcosm, which is modelled on the macrocosm, the great universe. The zodiac and the physical planets as well as the extrasensory planetary spheres play a major role in anthroposophy. Rudolf Steiner's clearly negative opinion on astrology, which deals with the zodiac and the planets, may therefore seem all the more surprising. In one of his many lectures, he commented on this as follows:

"The possibility of casting a horoscope is based on the truth that the one who has precise knowledge of these things can 'read' the forces according to which man finds his way into physical existence. Each of us is assigned a certain horoscope because in it the forces are expressed that have led us into this life. For example, if Mars is above Aries in a horoscope, this means that certain Aries forces cannot pass through Mars. They are weakened. Thus, the human being is placed into physical existence, and the horoscope is what he is guided by before he enters life on earth. This matter, which seems so daring in our day, should not be discussed **without pointing out that almost everything that is nowadays practiced in this area is the purest dilettantism – a true superstition – and that, as far as the world at large is concerned, the true science of these things has largely been lost! Therefore, the principals presented here should not be judged according to the claims of modern astrology, which is highly questionable."

After this radical distancing from the kind of astrology practiced today, Rudolf Steiner explained the connection between the human being and the cosmos.

"The active forces of the starry world push us into physical incarnation. Clairvoyant perception allows us to see in a person's organization that he or she is indeed the result of the working together of such cosmic forces. I want to illustrate this in a hypothetical form that nevertheless corresponds fully to clairvoyant perceptions.

If we took out a person's physical brain and examined its structure clairvoyantly and could see that certain functions are located in certain places and give rise to certain processes, we would find that each person's brain is different. No two people have the same brain. But just imagine, if we could photograph this brain with its entire structure, so that you would get a kind of hemisphere and all its details would be visible, this would provide a different picture from every person. And if we photographed a person's brain at the moment of birth and took a picture of the sky directly above his or her birthplace, the two pictures would be alike. The stars in the photograph of the sky would be arranged in the same way as certain parts of the brain in the other picture. Thus, our brain is really a picture of the heavens, and we each have a different picture depending on where and when we were born. This indicates that we are born out of the entire universe." [4]

As early as September 1905, when the later Anthroposophical Society was still part of the Theosophical Society as the "German Section", Rudolf Steiner answered the question "How does Theosophy relate to astrology?" with an unequivocal judgment:

---

[4] GA 15 "Die geistige Führung des Menschen und der Menschheit" (The Spiritual Guidance of the Individual and Humanity), Copenhagen (Denmark), lecture three, 8 June 1911. The stenographic transcript of the lectures was revised for publication by Rudolf Steiner himself.

"It must first be said that at present very little is known about what astrology really is. For what now often appears as such in manuals is a purely external compilation of rules, the deeper reasons for which are hardly ever given in any way. Methods of calculation are given by which certain constellations at the moment of a person's birth can be determined, or for the time of some other important matter. Then it is said that these constellations mean this or that, without being able to infer from the hints as to why all this is so, or only how it could be so. It is therefore no wonder that people of our age consider all this to be nonsense, hoax and superstition. Because it all appears to be a completely arbitrary assertion pulled purely out of thin air. At the most, it is generally said that everything in the world must be connected, that the positions of the Sun, Venus and Moon and so on in relation to each other at birth could very well have an effect on a person's life, and other such things.

However, real astrology is a completely intuitive science and requires the development of higher extrasensory powers of cognition in those who wish to practise it, which very few people can have today. And if one wants to explain its basic character, it is necessary to deal with the highest cosmological problems in the spiritual scientific sense. For this reason, only a few very general points of view can be given here."* [5]

Following these words, Rudolf Steiner went on to discuss the extrasensory forces at work in our solar system. He called it the "star system" at the time, because from an astronomical point of view our sun is a star.

---

[5] GA 34 "Lucifer-Gnosis 1903 – 1908", section "Questions and Answers"

"The star system to which we humans belong is a whole. And the human being is connected with all the forces of this star system. Only gross materialism can believe that the human being is only connected with the earth. You only have to look at the relationship between man, the sun and the moon in the results of the 'Akashic Records'. [6] *From this, one will see that there was a primeval development of man during which his dwelling place was a world body that still consisted of the sun, moon and earth together."*

Natural science refers to this primeval state of our solar system as the "primordial nebula". According to anthroposophical terminology, it existed during the first two great epochs of the earth's development, the so-called "polar epoch" and the subsequent "hyperborean epoch". Of course, the human being did not yet have a physical body at that time. However, he was already present in an astral-etheric primordial state, albeit without consciousness of himself. Later times called this primeval human state "Adam Kadmon", which means "primordial man".

In the course of the Hyperborean epoch, a gradual differentiation of the primordial nebula of our solar system took place. The sun contracted more and more, thereby separating the individual planets from itself.

"Therefore, even today man still has forces in his being that are related to those of the heavenly bodies mentioned. According to these affinities, there is also a connection that still exists today between the effects of the heavenly bodies mentioned and what happens in the

---

[6] The "Akashic Records", located in an extrasensory region, are a kind of comprehensive cosmic memory, which includes all events of evolution as well as all the experiences of human and higher beings. The development of a high level of consciousness is required in order to be able to "read" the Akashic Records.

human being. However, these effects are very different from those of a purely material nature, of which only modern science speaks. The sun, for example, also affects people through something quite different from what science calls attraction, light and warmth. There are extrasensory relationships between Mars, Mercury and other planets and the human being as well. On this basis, those who are predisposed to do so can form an idea of a web of extrasensory relationships between the heavenly bodies and the beings who inhabit them. But to elevate these relationships to clear and scientific knowledge **requires the development of the powers of a very high extrasensory vision! Only the highest degrees of Intuition still attainable by man can reach it!** [...]

There have been and still are people in occult schools who are able to practise astrology in this sense. And what is written about it in accessible books did in some way originate from such occult teachers. **However, everything that deals with these things is inaccessible to the common mind, even if it is written in books. Because understanding them, requires deep Intuition as well!**

And what has been written based on actual statements of the teachers by those who did not understood it themselves is, of course, not suitable for creating a favorable opinion of astrology in people who are caught up in the current way of thinking. But it must be said that even such books on astrology are not completely worthless. Because, the less people understand what they copy, the better they copy it. Then they do not spoil it with their own wisdom. Thus it is that in astrological writings, no matter how dark their origin, there are always pearls of truth to be found **by the one who is capable of Intuition – but only by him!**"

According to Rudolf Steiner's impressive statement, even the little that has been preserved by pure copying and without the writer's understanding can only be correctly interpreted and understood today by those who are capable of *"deep Intuition"* for which the *"powers of a very high extrasensory vision"* are required and which is completely extraordinary among today's humanity. Hardly any of the modern astrologers or authors of astrological books can claim with a clear conscience that they have achieved this necessary high level of extrasensory perception. And this certainly applies to the astrologers of the Middle Ages as well, and even those of ancient Greece, because even then the capability of spiritual vision had largely been lost. Only in the first half of the ancient Egyptian-Chaldean culture was it still widespread. In the second half, it declined more and more and finally faded away completely among certain peoples. This was particularly the case with those peoples who had a special task for humanity at the turn of the ages, such as the Hebrew people in connection with the incarnation of Christ and the Greeks and Romans with the subsequent spread of Christianity.

The numerous peoples of the earth all have their tasks and, with their respective characteristics, they contribute very special parts to the general development. The third post-Atlantean or post-glacial cultural period began around the year 3000 BC. Rudolf Steiner summarized its task with the words:

"Then follows the third period, the Egyptian-Chaldean-Babylonian one, in which the spirit continues to work. The sciences appear. The human being not only understands the world as a working field, but he searches for its laws. The Egyptian discovers geometry. The Chaldean searches in outer space for a pattern of the movements of the stars. The

world in its material substantiality, is thought to be pervaded by laws, that is, by spirit." [7]

In the first half of this period, people still had plenty of clairvoyant abilities, with the ancient Chaldeans and Babylonians being especially gifted in clairvoyant observation of the starry sky.

"The Chaldeans looked up to the heavens, and the light of the stars was not merely Maya for them; it was the script that the gods had imprinted on the physical plane. On the paths of the stars the Chaldean priest pursued the way back into the spiritual worlds, and when he was initiated, when he learned to know all the beings who inhabited the planets and the stars, he lifted up his eyes and said: What I see with my eyes when I gaze up to the heavens is the outer expression of what is given me by occult vision, by initiation. When the initiating priest endows me with the grace of the perception of the divine, then I see God. But all I see externally is not mere illusions; I see in it the handwriting of the gods." [8]

The Chaldeans' interpretation of this celestial writing was based on the still entirely spiritual cosmology that had been handed down to them by word of mouth from the previous Persian cultural period, based on the teachings of the great Zoroaster. They further developed this cosmology. They searched intensively for observable laws in the paths of the planets. In the 1st millennium BC, only excerpts of their extensive knowledge reached the public. The first astrological writings were created. Subsequently produced copies of

---

[7] GA 98 "Natur- und Geistwesen – ihr Wirken in unserer sichtbaren Welt" (Nature and Spirit Beings – Their Effects in Our Visible World), Munich, 29 April 1908

[8] GA 106 "Äyptische Mythen und Mysterien" (Egyptian Myths and Mysteries), Leipzig, lecture of 11 September 1908

varying quality finally reached Greece, where they became the basis of Greek astrology.

At that time, the most advanced part of humanity had matured to a new stage of development, to the formation of intellectual faculties. Rudolf Steiner therefore speaks of the dawning age of the intellectual soul. In order to develop this new ability, people needed to turn even more intensively to the physical sensory world than had previously been the case. For this purpose, the extrasensory perception had to be largely withdrawn from the peoples suited to the new development: the Greeks, Romans and Hebrews.

Among the Hebrew people, the prophets mentioned in the Old Testament initially still possessed various clairvoyant gifts. At the time when Yahweh demanded that Abraham sacrifice his son Isaac, Abraham possessed one last of these gifts. After he had shown himself willing to actually make this sacrifice, Yahweh stopped him, as the Old Testament reports. Instead of his son, he was to sacrifice a ram. Behind this story lies the sacrifice of the last psychic gift by Abraham so that his son Isaac could become the progenitor of the Hebrew people, who – among other tasks – were to make a special contribution to the development of the intellectual soul, undisturbed by psychic perceptions.

"This old Hebrew people had to give up bit by bit the old clairvoyance, which the other civilisations comprised within themselves. The old clairvoyance was bound to faculties which originated in the spiritual world. These clairvoyant faculties were designated, according to their nature, by expressions derived from starry images. The last faculty which was given up, in order to bestow the old Hebrew people on Abraham, was the one connected with the starry image of the Ram. Therefore a ram was sacrificed in place of Isaac. That is the external

expression for the sacrifice of the last clairvoyant power so that the old Hebrew people could be bestowed on Abraham. Thus, this people was chosen to develop just those powers which are aimed at the observation of the outer world." [9]

Two days later, Rudolf Steiner continued his explanations:

"Every gift from the spiritual world had to be renounced. The last gift from the spiritual world, which still remains when all previous ones have been darkened, is denoted in mystical symbolism by the ram. The two horns of the ram signify the sacrifice of the two-leaved lotus flower. [10] *The last clairvoyant gift is sacrificed after the earlier ones have already been discarded. In order to preserve this organization of the corporeality of Isaac, the last clairvoyant ability, the gift of Aries, the two-leaved lotus flower is sacrificed here.*

Then the Hebrews continue their mission in such a way that precisely these Abrahamic abilities are propagated from generation to generation. At the moment when this gift of clairvoyance reappears atavistically, when someone again sees into the spiritual worlds, such a reaction asserts itself that this person is expelled, that it is not tolerated within the community of the people. The antipathy towards this gift of the Ram manifests itself in hostility. This can be seen with Joseph. In his dreams he had prophetic illuminations from the spiritual world. He is quite naturally pushed out of his people because his faculty fell outside the actual mission of the Hebrews. He was rejected by his brothers

---

[9] GA 117 "Die tieferen Geheimnisse des Menschheitswerdens im Lichte der Evangelien" (Deeper Secrets of Human Evolution Viewed in the Light of the Gospels), Munich, lecture of 7 December 1909

[10] The "lotus flowers" are astral sensory organs that enable extrasensory perception. The "two-leaved lotus flower" is located at the forehead between the eyebrows. The structure of the human head is brought about by the forces of the zodiacal image of Aries (Ram).

because an heirloom of an old gift of clairvoyance reappeared in him. That is why Joseph had to go to Egypt. He fell out of the mission of his people." [11]

Unlike Joseph, Abraham was predisposed in his corporeality to perceive primarily through the physical brain. It was precisely this faculty that he was to pass on.

"Humanity was to acquire the ability to perceive through its brain. For this purpose the person had to be selected who had the most suitable brain, who was least predisposed to clairvoyant suggestions, but who could use the brain. Here again, we have one of the cases where reading of the Akashic Records confirms the facts of the Bible. What is written in the Bible is correct down to the letter. [12] *In fact, a person was chosen who, in his physical organization, had the most suitable brain to establish that which enabled spiritual work by means of the brain. This person was Abraham. He was chosen to fulfill the mission that would enable people to perceive the outside world through their physical brain. He was a person who was least suited to have any intuition, but who logically investigated external phenomena by measure, number and weight. An older tradition regards Abraham as the inventor of mathematics, and it is more right than today's public realises."* [13]

At around the same time, another people was tasked with developing rational philosophizing and logic. This mission was devolved on the Greeks. In the 4th century BC, the great philosopher

---

[11] GA 117 "Die tieferen Geheimnisse des Menschheitswerdens im Lichte der Evangelien" (Deeper Secrets of Human Evolution Viewed in the Light of the Gospels), Munich, lecture of 9 December 1909

[12] However, the ability is required to correctly *interpret* what is written, because many statements in the Bible are formulated as images or parables.

[13] Ibidem, Zürich (Switzerland), lecture of 19 November 1909

Aristotle could no longer resort to his own extrasensory perceptions, in contrast to his teacher Plato. Rudolf Steiner explains that Aristotle's writings are so extremely difficult for us to interpret today *"because Aristotle worked with a system of concepts that can be referred to an extrasensory world, but he no longer had a view of it."* [14]

However, Aristotle was by no means the only one of his time who lacked the gift of clairvoyance. The astronomers or astrologers of ancient Greece also no longer had their own extrasensory perceptions. They wrote their books by means of intellectual processing of old traditions still based on extrasensory perception, mainly from ancient Chaldea and Babylonia. But, much of what they found in the copies was no longer understood correctly and was therefore misinterpreted. As a result, a wide variety of errors crept into the early astrological teachings of the Greeks. These eventually became part of traditional astrology and have persisted to this day.

Much of the already erroneous Greek writings were in turn misinterpreted and thus mistranslated by later translators, both in the Middle Ages and today. In the end, all that remained led Rudolf Steiner to the above-mentioned judgment ***"that almost everything that is nowadays being practised in this direction is the purest dilettantism – a true superstition – and that for the outer world the true science of these things has largely been completely lost."***

"Almost everything", says Rudolf Steiner. Only the rudimentary remains and a lot of false ideas.

---

[14] GA 187 "Wie kann die Menschheit den Christus wiederfinden – Das dreifache Schattendasein unserer Zeit" (How Can Humanity Find the Christ Again? – The Triple Shadowy Existence of Our Time), Dornach, lecture of 25 December 1918

*"Do you really think a modern astrologer delving into ancient astrological writings to cast horoscopes – **and it is good if he** [only] **searches in the old writings, and does not produce any new ones; the new ones are terrible!** – has, in his abstraction, in his abstract way of thinking, even the slightest idea of the living connection which the ancient Egyptians and Chaldeans felt to exist between human beings and the movements and positions of the stars viewed from the earth? Everything has changed."* [15]

With the words quoted above: *"and it is good if he* [today's astrologer] [only] *searches in the old writings and **does not produce any new ones; the new ones are terrible"***, we may assume that Rudolf Steiner had previously familiarized himself with contemporary astrological teachings up to the year 1920, as he always did before giving a lecture on a particular subject. He could obviously only come to the conclusion that this was to a large extent "dilettantism" and "superstition".

Even the basic astrological work "Tetrabiblos" by the Greek geographer, mathematician and astronomer/astrologer Claudius Ptolemy from the 2nd century AD, which still has a decisive influence on today's astrology, is based solely on the astrological knowledge of that time, which already differed significantly from the astrology of the ancient Chaldeans, which was still based on extrasensory perception. At the time of Ptolemy, astrology was already mainly based on mental combinations and constructions. In a similar way, even today some astrologers try to create beautiful sets of rules and some of them develop really impressive astrological or astrosophical systems. However, there are few references to reality here, as the

---

[15] GA 197 "Gegensätze in der Menschheitsentwicklung" (Polarities in the Evolution of Mankind), Stuttgart, lecture of 5 March 1920

foundations from ancient Greece were only written down more than a millennium after the end of the Chaldean cultural epoch and were already full of errors. Anyone who fails to take this into account cherishes an illusion.

Rudolf Steiner's statements quoted above reflect his impressive judgment that today no one is able to develop a reality-based astrology or astrosophy who has not ascended, through many years of inner development, to the highest level of extrasensory perception, which he called "Intuition". Of course, this should not be confused with the emotional inner feeling for which we often use the same term in everyday language.

The gradual decline of knowledge of the zodiac

Today's concept of the zodiac has little in common with the original knowledge of the ancient Persians, Chaldeans and Babylonians. Over the last three millennia, this knowledge has gradually decayed. The reason for this is the loss of people's ancient clairvoyant abilities. The real zodiac was never visible to physical eyes. It was once seen psychically.

The clairvoyant vision of the extrasensory zodiacal images

Today we understand the term "zodiac" to mean the twelve constellations of stars that line up along the annual path of the sun in the sky, the so-called ecliptic. For this purpose, we combine groups of neighboring stars with lines to form abstract geometric figures and give them names that correspond roughly to those that the ancient Persians, Chaldeans and Babylonians bestowed on their clairvoyantly observed "zodiacal images". We no longer distinguish between the physically visible star constellations on the one hand and the zodiacal images once seen clairvoyantly by humans on the other. Both were merged with each other in the Greco-Roman cultural period, because there was no one left who was still able to see the real, extrasensory zodiacal images clairvoyantly, and furthermore because it was precisely the task of Greek culture to direct the people's consciousness entirely to the physical sensory world. As a result, the original knowledge of the psychic images of the zodiac was soon lost. The Greeks equated these images with constellations of stars, which they assumed to be in those directions in which the ancient Chaldeans once saw the clairvoyant images of the zodiac. In this way, a great misunderstanding crept into the Greek astrology.

The ancient pre-Greek peoples of the Near East would have been very surprised by the views of the later Greeks, and even more so by the abstract geometric figures that we use today in order to combine the corresponding groups of stars into constellations, because at the time when the zodiacal images could still be seen extrasensorily, such lines were not needed.

Both the ideas of the zodiac and the structure of our planetary system were originally of a completely different nature to those we have today. The very first cosmological teachings trace back to the great initiate Zarathustra or Zoroaster, who lived in the ancient Persian cultural period in the 5th millennium BC. The people of that time still had quite clear clairvoyance, by means of which they could perceive beings that do not have a physically visible body like humans, but only densify to an etheric or astral state imperceptible to the physical senses. In order to be able to see such beings, etheric-astral sensory organs were needed as "soul eyes": the "lotus flowers" mentioned in the previous chapter.

Thus, people could communicate with extrasensory beings and seek advice from them. They also had memories of an existence between two incarnations in which they lived together with these beings in higher worlds. As real as the peoples of other countries are to us today, as real were beings of higher planes of existence to the ancient Persians. They experienced them as entities of various levels of development and ruling over different areas of the higher worlds. In Christianity, the memory of them has been preserved as the doctrine of the "heavenly hosts". They are not referred to as "gods", but as "angelic hierarchies" of diverse ranks.

Zarathustra taught his disciples that the more developed these beings are, the further their realms extend from the earth into space. He described their realms as hollow spheres bounded by the orbits of the seven "planets" Moon, Mercury, Venus, Sun, Mars, Jupiter and Saturn, i.e. the seven visible celestial bodies which, unlike the fixed stars, follow their own orbits in the sky and were therefore called "wandering stars".

Immediately adjacent to the seventh and highest planetary sphere, as Zarathustra taught, is the zodiac of our solar system, which is inhabited by creative beings who rule over the order of the planetary spheres within the zodiac. In Christian terminology, they are called Cherubim.

Beyond the zodiac, there was a ninth, tenth and eleventh sphere (see the illustration from Schedel's World Chronicle of 1493). The latter was regarded as the abode of the supreme deity. These three spheres were called "crystal heaven" (Latin: Cristallinum), "first mover" (Primum Mobile), which was responsible for setting all development in the world in motion, and "fire heaven" (Empyrean – Empyreum) as the highest sphere.

In anthroposophical terminology, these four highest spheres – the zodiac and the three spheres above it – correspond to the 4th to 7th regions of the spiritual world. They are usually referred to collectively as the "higher spiritual world". In a narrower sense, this term is often only used for the three highest spheres because they are closely connected with the triune Godhead of our solar system: the 5th region with the Holy Spirit, the 6th region with the Son and the 7th region with the Father.

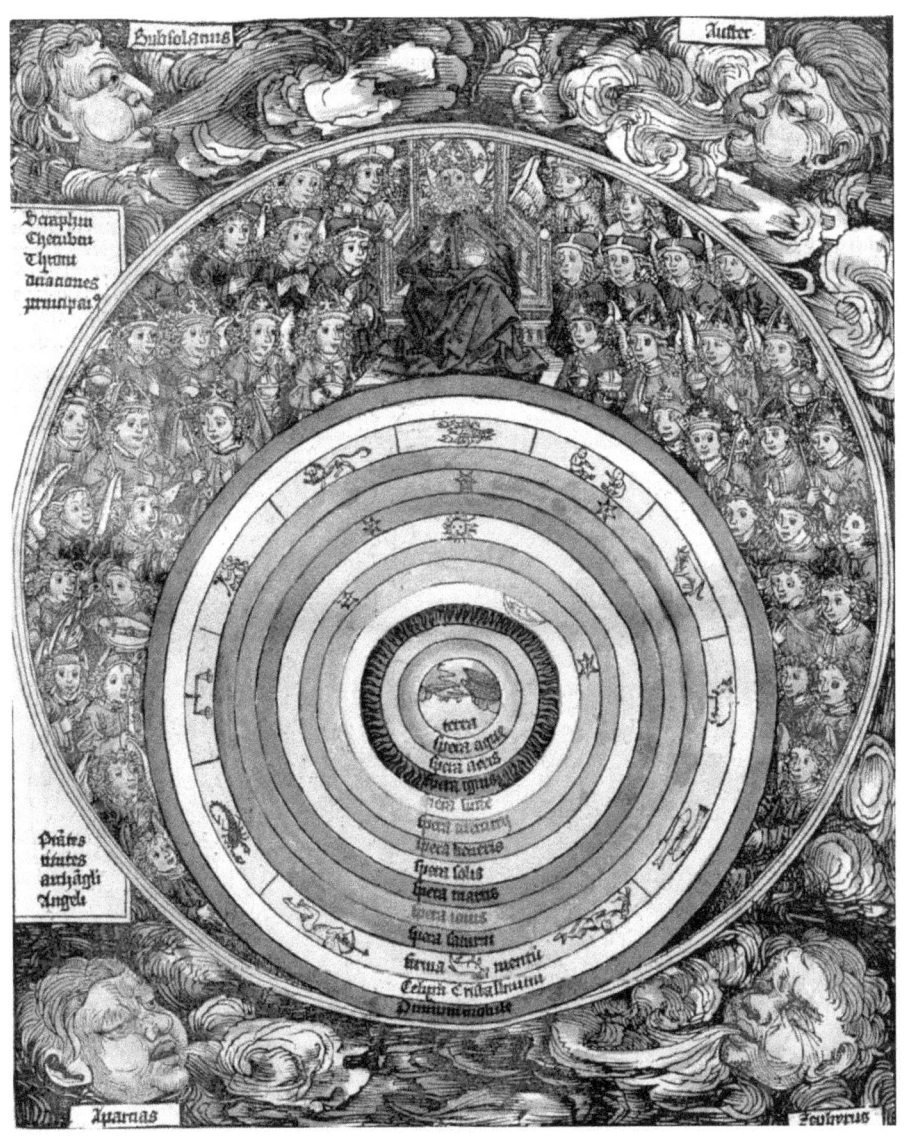

Figure 1:
The spheres of our solar system
in Schedel's World Chronicle (1493)

The triune deity once gave rise to three large groups of angelic beings, each of which is also tripartite. This means that a total of nine types of angels live in our solar system. Their names are given in the illustration in the left-hand margin, some of them in abbreviated form: "Seraphim, Cherubim, Thrones, Dominationes, Principatus, Potestates, Virtutes, Archangeli, Angeli". In contrast to the older order of the angelic hierarchies by Dionysius the Areopagite, a student of St. Paul, the names Principatus and Virtutes are interchanged. Rudolf Steiner refers to the beings of the second trinity below the thrones as Spirits of wisdom, movement and form, and the angelic beings of the third trinity as Archaï, Archangels and Angels.

The exalted Cherubim are beings of the zodiac. They live in the 8th sphere. The Seraphim live in the 9th sphere, in the direct sight of God and in cooperation with the Holy Spirit. According to His instructions, they organize and structure the spheres together with the Cherubim of the zodiac. In the 10th sphere, the Son sets all development in creation in motion. And in the 11th sphere are the origin and goal of the current cycle of creation.

Rudolf Steiner told us how the Cherubim revealed themselves to people in ancient times as beings of the zodiac:

"These great universal helpers appeared in quite definite etheric forms. Our forefathers, still conscious of these important facts through tradition, represented the Cherubim as strangely winged beasts with variously shaped heads: The winged Lion, the winged Eagle, the winged Bull and the winged Man.

For the Cherubim, in fact, first drew near from four sides. They approached in shapes that could afterwards be represented and thus become known as the forms of the Cherubim. Therefore, in schools of the first post-Atlantean initiates, the Cherubim, who approached the ancient Sun from four sides were given names which were later developed to the names Bull, Lion, Eagle and Man. [...]

The shapes of our present animals, even if they are distorted into caricatures today, were drawn forth from the periphery of the cosmos, from the forms of the zodiac that existed at that time. You may have noticed that initially only four names of the zodiac have been written here. They represent the principal expressions of the Cherubim, but in reality each of these cherubic beings has to the right and the left of it a kind of descendant or companion. If you think of each of the four cherubic figures as having two companions, then you have twelve forces and powers in the Sun's periphery which were already present in a certain sense with ancient Saturn. **We have twelve such powers belonging to the realm of the Cherubim** *who have to fulfill their task, their mission in the universe in the way we have said."* [16]

While in the depiction of Schedel's World Chronicle (Fig. 1, page 27) the earth is at the center and the sphere of God envelops creation on the outside, John, the favorite disciple of Jesus, experienced all that exactly the opposite in his great vision, which he tells us about in chapter 4 of his "Revelation". John was initiated by Christ himself. This enabled him to see into the four spheres of the higher spiritual world. He saw them in a unified image. At the center he saw the throne of God, surrounded by the four most important beings of the 8th sphere, the cherubim of the zodiac. But he also saw the crystal heaven, the 9th sphere, and described it with the words:

"Before the throne there was a sea of glass, like crystal. And in the midst of the throne, and around the throne, were four living creatures full of eyes in front and in back. The first living creature was like a lion,

---

[16] GA 110 "Geistige Hierarchien und ihre Widerspiegelung in der physischen Welt" (Spiritual Hierarchies and their Reflections in the Physical World), Düsseldorf, lecture of 13 April 1909, in the evening

the second living creature like a calf, the third living creature had a face like a man, and the fourth living creature was like a flying eagle. The four living creatures, each having six wings, were full of eyes around and within." (Rev. 4:6-8)

The zodiac region also contains the so-called Akashic Records, in which all events in the history of the earth and the individual stages of development of all humans since the beginning of creation are recorded. It is the "book of life". Karma is formed on its basis. John saw the Akashic Records pictorially in the form of a book or a sealed scroll:

"And I saw in the right hand of Him who sat on the throne a scroll written inside and on the back, sealed with seven seals." (Rev. 5:1)

In the vision, the scroll also represented the omniscience of God over every detail of creation. It is an expression of the Holy Spirit, the third divine person.

John saw the second divine person, the Son, in the form of a lamb, who alone is worthy to open the seals of the book:

"The Lamb came forward and took the scroll from the right hand of the one who was seated on the throne. When he had taken the scroll, the four living creatures and the twenty-four elders prostrated themselves before the Lamb. Each of the elders was holding a harp, and they had gold bowls filled with incense, which are the prayers of the saints. They sang a new song: You are worthy to receive the scroll and to open its seals, for you were slain, and with your blood you purchased for God people of every tribe and language, nation and race. You have made them to kings and priests to serve our God, and they will reign on earth." (Rev. 5:8-10)

As we can see, the ancient world view from the times of Zarathustra persisted well into our Christian era and was generally accepted. Even today, believers still regard the Revelation of John as the most profound and highly spiritual document of Christianity.

However, it is no longer appreciated by all those who have since turned their full attention to the physical outside world. Now that the possibility of seeing higher spheres and beings has been lost, solely intellectual thinking is used. The traditions of ancient cultures are dismissed by many as fantasy or superstition. A purely materialistic view of the world has prevailed and is presented as the only realistic one. This opinion is supported by the fact that very few people today have any access to the higher worlds and their inhabitants, during life on earth.

However, the situation is quite different in the period between two incarnations. After death we expand as soul-spiritual beings into the extrasensory planetary spheres and even spheres above. There we work out our karma and take part in building the spiritual archetype of our future body for a new life on earth. Rudolf Steiner described the individual stages of this process, which generally extends over many centuries, several times.[17]

When we incarnated thousands of years ago in ancient Persia, Egypt, Chaldea or Babylonia, we still brought with us very vivid memories of our experiences in the spheres between the last death and a new birth. Life after death was something we all took for granted. In the beginning, we still had a full overview of our incarnation cycle and could even look back on previous incarnations. Over the millennia, our memories became fainter until they finally ceased completely in the Greco-Roman cultural epoch. As a result, the Western world (including Europe) not only lost the knowledge of

---

[17] See e.g. footnote 3 (page 7) as well as the author's book "The Anthroposophical Soul Calendar and the Incarnation Cycle of Man", Publisher BoD (Books on Demand), Norderstedt (Germany)

reincarnation, but also of an existence before birth, the so-called pre-existence of the soul. In the Eastern world, this knowledge has survived longer. However, over the course of time it has also been distorted, falsified and richly embellished with pictorial fantasies. Today it bears only a remote resemblance to the ancient knowledge. The doctrine of reincarnation was even degraded to the doctrine of the "transmigration of souls", according to which humans would also return as animals.

According to the occult principle "As in the great, so in the small" the extrasensory planetary spheres have material images in the physical planets of our solar system, whereby their orbits mark the boundaries of the spheres. Similarly, our pre-natal experiences in the spheres during the long time between two incarnations have an earthly image in the individual stages of our life on earth. In the book *"The Mirroring of Life before Birth in the Seven-Year Periods of Human Life on Earth"*[18], the author has illustrated this fact with examples from his own life. However, anyone who fundamentally rejects the possibility of a pre-birth existence of the human soul in higher regions will probably not find access to such connections in his life.

From the perspective of today's prevailing material world view, the universe consists only of physical solar systems, because every star that shines in the night sky is a sun. Many of these, if not most, are surrounded by planets.

From the perspective of the world view of ancient cultures, every sun, like its planets, arises from a zodiac. It is a circle of forces invisible to the physical eye. Contrary to the assumption of modern astrology, the zodiac is not identical with the distant stars or even constellations, but is part of the outer region of each solar system. According to Rudolf Steiner, all solar systems that we see as shining

---

[18] Publisher BoD (Books on Demand), Norderstedt (Germany)

stars in the night sky are colonies of spiritual beings. To be able to recognize this, however, one must have developed the highest level of extrasensory perception: Intuition.

"For physical sight the stars are points of radiance at the boundaries of the space in the direction towards which we are looking. If we have acquired the faculty of Intuitive Knowledge, the stars are the revealers of cosmic Beings, spiritual Beings. And with Intuition we behold in the spiritual Universe, instead of the physical stars, colonies of spiritual Beings at the places where we conceive the physical stars to be situated." [19]

Each solar system, each colony of spiritual beings, has its own supreme triune deity who, with the help of exalted angelic beings, builds up the planetary system and guides its development.

"Thus, we must see as beyond the Seraphim the supreme Divinity, which we find as threefold Divinity among most peoples, expressed as Brahma, Shiva and Vishnu, as the Father, the Son and the Holy Ghost. The creative source of a new cosmic system also resides within this lofty Trinity. Looking back to ancient Saturn, we may say that before anything of it came into existence the plan for it had to ripen within the divine Trinity. But this divine Trinity needs beings to execute its plan and these beings must first prepare themselves for the task. The Seraphim, Cherubim and Thrones are the beings who are, so to speak, closest to the Godhead. In Western Christian esotericism they are appropriately described as 'enjoying the unveiled countenance of the Godhead.' They receive the plans of a new cosmic system from the divine Trinity from whom they originated." [20]

---

[19] GA 239 "Esoterische Betrachtungen karmischer Zusammenhänge" (Karmic Relationships V), Paris, lecture of 23 May 1924

[20] GA 110 "Geistige Hierarchien und ihre Widerspiegelung in der physischen Welt" (Spiritual Hierarchies and their Reflections in the Physical World), Düsseldorf, lecture of 14 April 1919, in the evening

The Seraphim, who inhabit the 9th sphere, are also the ambassadors between the various cosmic systems or planetary systems in the universe. Rudolf Steiner explained:

"So, in a similar way there is communication between one planetary system and another by means of the Seraphim. They are, as it were, to the whole system, that which on earth corresponds to the speech which draws people together, holds them together, and leads them to understanding. The Seraphim carry messages from one planetary system to another, and give information of what takes place in one planetary system to the other system." [21]

Every planetary system not only arises within a zodiac, but also develops higher and higher until it finally becomes a new zodiac itself.

"This is followed by the Vulcan condition, the highest stage in the development of our system. The seven stages in the evolution of our system, therefore, are: Saturn, Sun, Moon, Earth, Jupiter, Venus and Vulcan. During the Vulcan stage all the beings who have evolved out of the small beginnings of Saturn will have been spiritualized in the highest degree. Together they will have grown not only to being a sun, but more than a sun. Vulcan is more than a sun, and it will have reached the maturity of sacrifice, the maturity necessary for self-disintegration.

This is the next stage of development, that such a system, in which a sun arises from a starting point, this sun is first weak, so to speak, and has to throw out its planets so that it can develop itself further. It

---

[21] GA 136 "Die geistigen Wesenheiten in den Himmelskörpern und Naturreichen" (Spiritual Beings in the Heavenly Bodies and in the Kingdoms of Nature), Helsingfors (Helsinki, Finland), lecture of 10 April 1912

becomes strong, integrates its planets again, becomes Vulcan. And now the whole thing dissolves, and the Vulcan sphere later becomes a hollow sphere; it then becomes something similar to this circle of Thrones, Cherubim and Seraphim. So the sun will dissolve, sacrifice itself out into the universe, radiate its essence. And thereby it will itself become a circle of such beings as the Seraphim, Cherubim and Thrones are, which now progresses to new creation in the universe." [22]

Rudolf Steiner describes here a phenomenon that our astronomers explain as the explosion of a star at the end of its life cycle, whereby a "stella nova" (Latin for new star) or simply a "nova" becomes visible in the sky. From a physical point of view, this is the transition of a planetary system from its Vulcan stage to a new zodiac, from which a new planetary system will emerge after a long time. This is what is meant by "progresses to new creation" in the above quote.

"An ancient solar system has disappeared and faded away. Within this ancient system the circles of the Seraphim, Cherubim, Thrones have attained their highest perfection. Now, in accordance with the indications of the supreme Trinity, they choose a sphere within cosmic space and say: let us begin here. Then, the Seraphim receive the aims of this new solar system, the Cherubim work them out, and the Thrones let the primordial fire flow out of their own being into this spherical space." [23]

Today's astronomers do not speak of "primordial fire", but of "primordial nebula", which is one level denser. They assume that this was divided into individual planets and our sun, as a result of solely

---

[22] GA 110 "Geistige Hierarchien und ihre Widerspiegelung in der physischen Welt" (Spiritual Hierarchies and their Reflections in the Physical World), Düsseldorf, lecture of 14 April 1919, in the evening

[23] Ibidem

physical laws, that living beings then emerged from the initially dead material through a series of "coincidences" and that at some point consciousness flared up in them, which developed into the human mind.

The initiates of early antiquity, on the other hand, did not experience this creative process as random, but as wisely planned and guided by highest beings, who are far above humanity and who influence the inner space and the earth from the outer area of our planetary system, from the zodiacal region, from twelve directions. Rudolf Steiner described this experience as follows:

"People have, indeed, no idea today of the way in which humans once, in ancient times, when an instinctive clairvoyance still persisted among them, gazed out into the cosmos. People believe today that the various drawings, pictures, imaginations, which were made of the zodiacal signs, were the products of fantasy. They are not. They were sensed, they were seen by facing the cosmos. Human progress required the damping-down of this instinctive, living, Imaginative perception, in order that intellectual perception, which sets us free, should come in its place, from which, however, if we want to be real human beings, such a view of the universe again be attained, which in turn advances to Imagination, but now with full consciousness, no longer instinctively." [24]

Rudolf Steiner went on to explain that the extrasensory images or Imaginations of the twelve directions of space do not belong to the three-dimensional space within which we experience ourselves in our present waking consciousness, but to an extrasensory two-dimensional planar space:

---

[24] GA 82 "Damit der Mensch ganz Mensch werde" (So that the Human Being can Become Fully Human), The Hague, lecture of 9 April 1922

*"If one wants to come in this way from the starry sky to a conception of space, then one does not get a space which encompasses three dimensions, but one gets a space which I can only indicate pictorially: If I had to indicate the space of which I spoke yesterday by the three lines standing perpendicular to each other [in the center of figure 2], I would have to indicate this other space in such a way that I would draw such configurations everywhere, as if forces in **planes** approached the earth from all sides of the universe and from the outside had a plastic effect on the formations which are on the surface of the earth.*

*One arrives at such an idea when one advances from what can be seen with the physical eyes in living beings, above all in human beings, to what I have now called Imagination, whereby the cosmos reveals to one in image form instead of the physical human being and gives one **a new space**."*

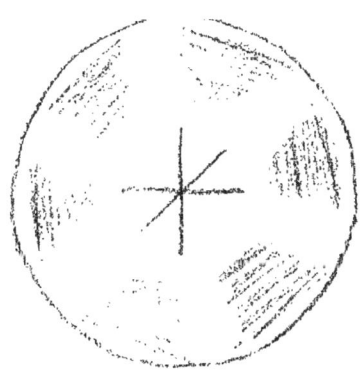

Figure 2:
Rudolf Steiner's sketch on the two-dimensional spatial areas of the zodiac

Explaining this, Rudolf Steiner drew the above sketch on the blackboard. It shows six shaded areas of equal size opposite each other, representing the twelve areas of force in the space surrounding the earth. According to this, we should be able to assume that all areas of force are the same size.

Looking at the different points of the compass triggered different images in the souls of the ancient Persians, Chaldeans and Babylonians, always depending on the respective cardinal direction. These images have come down to us as the zodiacal images. They could be "seen" again and again. This is why people initially did not need any physically visible signs in the sky to mark the respective directions of space.

But the ancient clairvoyance had to fade in order that people could be detached from the guidance of the higher beings of our solar system and achieve freedom and develop I-consciousness. These are important tasks of the present age of the consciousness soul. It began in 1413. Until then, the ancient world view of the spheres and knowledge of the extrasensory beings of our solar system had been preserved.

"Even in the middle of the Middle Ages, people still knew this. They knew it to the extent of being able to paint it. In other words: It is not so long ago, that human beings were pushed completely on to the physical plane.

And what we are told today by materialistic world view as the course of the spiritual history of mankind is, after all, nothing but a deception, because people think that the human being has always been as he has become in the course of the past few centuries, whereas it is not very long ago that he used to look into the spiritual world by means of ancient clairvoyance. He only had to abandon the spiritual world, because he was not free, and in order to acquire full freedom and

I-consciousness, he had to get out of it. Now he must find his way back into the spiritual world. Therefore, Spiritual Science prepares something very important and essential: namely, this re-entry into the spiritual world." [25]

Probably no people felt the gradual fading of the old clairvoyance as tragically as the ancient Germanic tribes. When the Greeks and Hebrews had long since lost their formerly innate clairvoyance, there were still numerous persons among the Germanic tribes north of the Alps who were capable of extrasensory perception. They painfully experienced that they increasingly lost this gift and with it the ability to communicate with the higher beings under whose guidance and protection they felt themselves to be. In their great epic "Ragnarök", which means "fate of the gods", they impressively described the gradual loss of the ancient clairvoyance as the "downfall" of their world of gods. The composer Richard Wagner brought this process to the stage, entitled "Twilight of the Gods".

The widespread view today that the people of past eras were largely fantasists and dreamers, whereas only we today know exactly what the world is really like, is the result of the immense arrogance of our intellectual age. The average person of the present day tends very strongly to believe that he or she is a truly enlightened person who sees the world as it really is, without all the "talk" of angels or other extrasensory beings. Unfortunately, the numerous, truly fantastic and fairytale-like stories of the ancient mythologies contribute to this misconception. However, they are only a final, fanciful embellished and allegorical expression of extrasensory experiences.

---

[25] GA 168 "Die Verbindung zwischen den Lebenden und den Toten" (Relationships Between the Living and the Dead), Leipzig, lecture of 22 Februar 1916

It is also easy to forget that the same ancient peoples who handed down their myths to us created extremely monumental buildings, such as the pyramids of Egypt, where even our experts have to admit that they cannot really explain, but at best only speculate, how the ancients managed to build such gigantic structures with their simple means. One thing is certain: they were definitely not fantasists. However, unlike us today, they were not yet completely limited to their physical "five senses". They were not as "narrow-sensed" and "narrow-minded" as we are today, but had other means of perception that gave them access to extrasensory regions.

The determination of individual stars as physically visible markers between the zodiacal images

In the second half of the Chaldean-Babylonian cultural period, which began around the year 3000 BC, the ancient clairvoyance of the peoples of the Near East was already very much in decline. This made it necessary for them to determine physically visible objects in order to use them as markers of the boundaries between the spatial areas of the clairvoyantly seen, but now increasingly fading, zodiacal images. To this end, the astronomers/astrologers of the time searched the sky for suitable stars. And so it came about that they named a star that was in the direction corresponding to the boundary between the clairvoyant zodiacal images of Taurus and Aries Hamal, the Arabic word for mutton, ram or lamb. This is how the first stars received their Arabic names. Others were added later.

The Greeks later called the star Hamal "α Arietis", which means the first star of Aries. However, it is not in 0° Aries, as one might mistakenly assume, but in 30° Aries, which is equivalent to 0° Taurus, because Hamal is the boundary marker between the extrasensory images of Taurus and Aries.

The Chaldeans and Babylonians dealt with other stars in a similar way. In the transition area from the image of Taurus to that of Gemini, they saw the brightly shining star Aldebaran. At that time, however, the Gemini were not yet seen as a pair of siblings, but as a human couple consisting of a man and a woman. They were still depicted in this form by the ancient Egyptians and Chaldeans. It was not until the Greeks that they were replaced by the twins Castor and Pollux, two figures from their own mythology. The star Regulus was seen near the border between the extrasensory images of Leo and Virgo. [26]

In this way, a connection was established for the first time between the zodiac, which could only be experienced clairvoyantly, and some physically visible objects in the starry sky. Initially, however, these were only individual stars and not yet constellations.

The zodiac is an invisible circle of forces that surrounds our planetary system and has a formative effect on it from twelve directions. Such an idea is of course hardly acceptable to our modern astronomers, because natural science at its present stage of development can only imagine forces emanating from material bodies. Even the forces that physicists describe as acting in atoms are thought of as associated with elementary particles of various kinds, i.e. with something material. Only the next stage in the development

---

[26] Further information can be found in the author's book "Influences of the Forces of the Zodiac on the Cultural Development of Mankind", Publisher BoD – Books on Demand, Norderstedt (Germany)

of natural science will bring the realization that there are also forces, even entities, that are not bound to any material substance.

The definition of twelve constellations to replace the spatial areas of the fading zodiacal images

For a long time, only some stars were of importance to the astronomers of antiquity; precisely those that served as visible markers between two zodiacal images. However, with the transition from the Egyptian-Chaldean-Babylonian period to the Greco-Roman period, astronomers began to designate entire groups of stars located between or around two boundary markers with the names of the extrasensory zodiacal images. In this way, they projected, solely mentally, the previously clairvoyantly seen images onto twelve physically visible constellations.

In order to determine the distances between the individual stars more precisely and to indicate their respective positions on the ecliptic, the Greek astrologers/astronomers devised lines between the stars. Over time, the line figures of the star constellations that are still known today came into being.

In addition, it was determined which star of a constellation should correspond to which part of a zodiacal image. For example, a star was thought to be located at the "mouth of the ram". And since the Greeks projected many figures from their own mythology onto the sky in a solely intellectual construction, there was also a star "at the left foot of Andromeda", and so on. In this way, the extrasensory images of the zodiac, which had long since ceased to be perceptible, were finally equated with the abstractly created constellations and replaced by them, although there was no direct connection. It was not the physically visible constellations that evoked the extrasensory zodiacal images in people's souls, but the objectless forces of the twelve directions of space. Thus the original, true knowledge of the zodiac had already been lost to the ancient Greeks. From then on, people spoke primarily of the constellations.

600 years after the beginning of the Greek cultural period, the Greek astronomer Hipparchus of Nicaea (ca. 190 to ca. 120 BC) endeavored to determine and record the positions of some stars more precisely with the help of imaginary connecting lines. A further 300 years later, almost a millennium after the beginning of the Greek cultural epoch, the great astronomer Claudius Ptolemy (approx. 100 to after 160 AD) reported in his "Almagest" how his predecessor Hipparchus had proceeded in determining the position of a star in the constellation of the Triangulum. This constellation is located above Aries. Hipparchus had noted: *"The preceding star (β Triangulum) on the base line of the Triangulum deviates one inch to the east from a straight line that passes through the star [α] at the mouth of Aries and that [γ] at the left foot of Andromeda."*

At that time, however, astronomers did not yet fully agree on the exact assignment of the stars to the individual parts of the zodiacal images projected onto the sky purely in their minds. Ptolemy, for example, was of the opinion that α Arietis was not located at the mouth of Aries but above its head, contrary to Hipparchus' opinion. In his catalog, Ptolemy therefore describes the star α Arietis with the words: *"The one above the head that Hipparchus places at the snout."*

However, the star constellations of the ancient Greeks did not coincide exactly with the clairvoyantly seen images of the zodiac.

Only the images had a causal connection with the forces of the zodiac, as they were ultimately brought about by these very forces in the human souls. No astrological statements can be derived from the visible constellations. This is a fundamental error. Rudolf Steiner therefore pointed out:

*"If one were simply to record what one sees out there in cosmic expanses, one would achieve nothing. **Simply mapping the starry sky, as today's astronomers do, leads nowhere.**"* [27]

Ultimately, this error led to a serious change in the old worldview. The depiction in Schedel's World Chronicle of 1493 (Fig. 1, page 27) shows the original knowledge of the zodiac forces. There, the twelve clairvoyant images are drawn in the 8th sphere, through which the Cherubim reveal themselves as inhabitants of the zodiac sphere. At the edge of the picture there is even the name "Cherubim", together with the names of the extrasensory inhabitants of the other spheres.

Just a few decades later, in 1525, the cartographer, mathematician and astronomer/astrologist Peter Apian[28] published a similar representation of the ancient worldview in his book "Cosmographicus Liber". Here, however, the starry sky has taken the place of the zodiacal images. The 8th sphere is called "Firmamentum". It was now imagined as a large, massive hollow sphere with fixed stars attached to its inner surface. Instead of the painted zodiacal images, only the abstract symbols ♈♉♊♋♌♍♎♏♐♑♒♓ are entered in the 8th sphere, together with a number of stars as an indication of constellations.

---

[27] GA 82 "Damit der Mensch ganz Mensch werde" (So that the Human Being can Become Fully Human), The Hague, lecture of 9 April 1922

[28] Peter Apian (1495 – 1552) from Leisnig in Saxony (a landlocked state of Germany), actually Peter Bennewitz or Bienewitz. The Latin word for German "Biene" (bee) is "apis".

Figure 3:
The spheres of our solar system
in the Cosmographia of Peter Apian (1539 edition)

In addition, the names of the nine angelic hierarchies were not listed by Peter Apian. As a result of the Reformation, the "heavenly hosts" lost their importance at that time. The Reformed churches largely rejected the worship of angelic beings. Only the supreme deity and the saints still mattered. Accordingly, Peter Apian only mentioned these in his illustration. Around the spheres he wrote: "COELUM EMPIREUM HABITACULUM DEI ET OMNIUM ELECTORUM", that is, "Empyrean Heaven [= fire heaven], abode of God and all the elect". Now, there was only God and humanity, and nothing in between.

When the purely material world view became dominant in the 19th century, people eventually began even to deny or at least seriously question the existence of God. The astronomers declared that they had found no God in the cosmos, which is not at all surprising since their search was limited to the material world. And, of course, no zodiac powers were found this way.

Ultimately, not only was the original knowledge of the zodiac lost, but our solar system was "depopulated" by all extrasensory beings. Only humans remained and the three lower kingdoms of nature: animals, plants and minerals. However, it is important to take into account that the denial of extrasensory levels of existence and the spiritual entities that inhabit them is only a few hundred years old. It is extremely young!

If we consider that fundamental changes to the "modern" world view occur approximately every 50 years due to new scientific findings, there is hope that natural science will lead to a spiritual science in the future. Then the part of humanity that is able to develop spiritually and whose world view is not blinded by material existence will no longer feel lonely in the cosmos, but will learn again to come into contact with the extrasensory inhabitants of our solar system. Until then, however, most people in the Western world will consider the ancient world view to have been overcome, and science is proud of it.

The non-consideration of the precession of the vernal equinox in Greek astrology

During the Greek cultural epoch, the prevailing doctrine was that the sun rose in Aries at the beginning of spring. However, the constellations, which were equated with the zodiac, did not correspond exactly with the spatial areas of the zodiacal images invisible to the physical eye.

A further complication was added by the slow shift of the sun's rising point at the beginning of spring. There was no definite knowledge about this either. It was difficult to obtain such knowledge, as the shift is only 1° every 72 years. Thus, it is hardly noticeable during a person's lifetime. There was also no tradition regarding this shift, when people had the old clairvoyance, they saw the images. There was no need to think about the rising point of the sun at the vernal equinox in an abstract mathematical way.

The observant Greek astronomer Hipparchus, who was still able to draw on some of his predecessors' notes, nevertheless noticed when evaluating the data available to him that a strange change was taking place in the sky over longer periods of time. However, he was not thinking of a shift of the vernal equinox in front of the fixed stars, but instead of a shift of the fixed stars themselves. However, there was great uncertainty as to how this was possible, given that the stars were firmly attached to the inside of the great celestial vault, as was believed, and to what extent or at what speed the shift would occur.

As Ptolemy reports, Hipparchus suspected that only the fixed stars close to the ecliptic would shift, but not the others. In the end,

Ptolemy at least agreed with Hipparchus' assumption that the vernal point would shift backwards by 1° over the course of 100 years. Today we know that this happens in the course of 72 years.

In several lectures, Rudolf Steiner gave an overview of the positions of the vernal equinox in the various eras of human development. In the lecture of January 16, 1920, he wrote the following dates on the blackboard to mark the beginning and end of the five post-Atlantean (post-glacial) cultural epochs up to now: [29]

I	Primeval Indian	from 8167 to 5567 BC
II	Primeval Persian	from 5567 to 2907 BC
III	Egyptian-Chaldean	from 2907 to 747 BC
IV	Greek-Latin	from 747 BC to 1413 AD
V	Now	from 1413 to ...

This results in a duration of 2,160 years for each of the ages III to V, but 2,660 years for age II, the primeval Persian or Gemini age, and 2,600 years for age I, the Primeval Indian or Cancer age. Deviating from this, in his sketch of the clairvoyantly seen zodiacal images (Figure 2, page 37) Rudolf Steiner drew all six areas the same size. Since they were certainly drawn to represent the twelve areas of the zodiac, we should initially assume that all ages last the same length of time.

However, it is possible that the vernal equinox moved more slowly during the primeval Persian and primeval Indian ages than during the next three ages. Something similar is observed in the Earth's orbit around the Sun. At the summer solstice, when the Sun passes through Gemini and Cancer as seen from the Earth, the Earth

---

[29] GA 196 "Geistige und soziale Wandlungen in der Menschheitsentwicklung" (Spiritual and Social Transformations in Human Development), Dornach

is furthest away from the Sun on its orbit and its speed is the slowest as a result. Therefore, it takes longer to pass through the two images. In the months before and after the winter solstice, on the other hand, when the Sun passes through Sagittarius and Capricorn, as seen from the Earth, the Earth is closest to the Sun and its speed is highest.

When Copernicus recognized in the 16th century the slow rotation of the Earth's axis as the cause of the precession of the vernal equinox, he also assumed that the rotation of the axis was not uniform, but of different speed. Only much later did it emerge that the fluctuations he had identified were due to inaccuracies in the measurements of the ancient astronomers on the basis of which he made his calculations. Unfortunately, it is not possible to directly observe and measure the precessional movement of the vernal equinox over long periods, but only to calculate it mathematically, taking into account traditional data. Modern astronomy assumes a uniform rotation of the earth's axis. But at the end, no matter how exact the calculation result, it is no guarantee that it corresponds to reality, as the example of Copernicus shows.

With regard to the Greek-Latin and Egyptian-Chaldean cultural epochs, Rudolf Steiner repeatedly emphasized:

"In 747, before the event of Golgotha, the vernal equinox entered the zodiac sign of Aries. It remained in this sign of the zodiac until the 15th century. Then it passed over and is now in the zodiacal image of Pisces. Before 747, the vernal equinox was in the sign of Taurus, so throughout the Egyptian-Chaldean cultural period the sun rose in the zodiacal image of Taurus in spring; hence the service of Taurus. The primeval Persian period was, when the sun rose in the zodiacal image of Gemini.

The sun rose in the zodiacal image of Cancer during the primeval Indian period." [30]

Thus, in the year 747 BC, the vernal equinox first moved from the spatial area of the extrasensory image of Taurus backwards into the spatial area of the image of Aries. At the beginning of the Greco-Roman era in 747 BC, it was therefore in 0° Taurus = 30° Aries. Over the course of the next 900 years, it moved a further 12.5° backwards through the spatial area of the Aries image and was therefore at 17.5° Aries during Ptolemy's lifetime, around the year 150 AD. Near this place are two stars in the sky that belong to the large constellation of Pisces. These are π Piscium (Pi Piscium[31]) and o Piscium (Omicron Piscium). Because these two stars coincided then with the sunrise point at the beginning of spring, Ptolemy assumed that 0° Aries was there. In his Almagest, he therefore gave the position 0° 10' ♈ for π Piscium and 0° 30' ♈ for o Piscium, although both are located at approximately 17° 30' ♈. [32]

Ptolemy's conception of the zodiac deviated by more than half a zodiacal image from the actual positions of the spatial areas of the zodiacal forces, which were only clairvoyantly ascertainable. In this way, two serious errors crept into astrology. Firstly, the definition of the rising point of the sun at the beginning of spring as the "Aries point" at 0° ♈ did not correspond to reality, because this point was located at 17° 30' ♈ at the time. Secondly, astrology ignores the shift of the vernal equinox.

---

[30] GA 205 "Menschenwerden, Weltenseele und Weltengeist – Teil 1" (Human evolution, World Soul and World Spirit), Dornach, lecture of 9 July 1921

[31] „Piscium" is the genitive plural of the Latin word Pisces for fish.

[32] Further information and two illustrations can be found in the author's book "Influences of the Forces of the Zodiac on the Cultural Development of Mankind", Publisher BoD (Books on Demand), Norderstedt (Germany)

Therefore, in all ephemerides we find the position of the sun at the beginning of spring entered as 0° ♈. According to Rudolf Steiner's information above, however, this only corresponds to reality for a few decades around the year 1413. In that year, the period of the sun's rising at the beginning of spring in the image of Aries ended. Since then it has risen in the zodiacal image of Pisces (not to be confused with the constellation).

Later astrologers caused additional confusion. They thought that when the vernal equinox was located at the stars π Piscium and o Piscium in Ptolemy's time, then it must have already been the Age of Pisces. They confused the visible constellations with the extra-sensory images of the zodiac. And because a new era had begun with the birth of Christ, only around 150 years before Ptolemy, and the early Christians used the fish as a symbol of Christ, this was also erroneously taken as evidence that the Piscean Age had begun at that time. However, the fish in connection with Christ only pointed to his task of preparing humanity for the following Piscean Age as early as the Age of Aries, in which He appeared as the "Lamb of God" and accomplished the Mystery of Golgotha.

There is similar confusion among some astrologers today regarding the Age of Aquarius. They claim that this has already begun or is imminent, whereas the vernal equinox will only enter the zodiacal image of Aquarius around the year 3573, moving backwards from Pisces, provided we assume a duration of 2,160 years also for the Age of Pisces. Since the year 1413, not even a third of the Age of Pisces has expired. So there are still two thirds to go.

Rudolf Steiner therefore repeatedly and unequivocally emphasized, even in 1923, two years before his death:

"Today the sun rises on the morning of 21 March at a point where it has the zodiacal **image** of the Fishes behind it. But if we go further back through history, for instance to the time before Christ was born, then the sun did not rise in the zodiacal **image** of the Fishes but in the **image** of the Ram. If we make a drawing, it is like this: If the sun rises in the Fishes in spring, on 21 March, nowadays, it rose in the Ram about 2160 years ago, and earlier than that in the Bull, and even earlier in the Twins." [33]

We can therefore state the following: At the time of Christ's birth, the sun rose at the beginning of spring within the boundaries of the image of the Ram or Aries, which can only be perceived by clairvoyance. In the distant background, far behind the **image** of the Ram or Aries, which is invisible to the physical eye, is the physically visible **constellation** of Pisces. However, this has nothing directly to do with the zodiac itself. If it had, the extrasensory image of two fish would have lit up in the souls of the ancient Persians, Chaldeans and Babylonians when they looked and sensed in this direction. Instead, however, they saw the image of an animal that resembled a ram.

It was not until 1413 that the vernal equinox reached 0° Aries = 30° Pisces. Since then, it has moved further into the area of the clairvoyantly seen image of the Fishes. In 2025, it will have moved 8.5° into this image and will therefore be at 30° ♓ - 8.5° = 21.5° ♓. When calculating a horoscope for a person born in the first decades of our century, this means that 8.5° must be subtracted from each of the planetary positions given in the ephemeris. This also applies to the Ascendant and all other house cusps.

---

[33] GA 349 "Vom Leben des Menschen und der Erde – Über das Wesen des Christentums" (On the Life of the Human Being and the Earth – On the Essence of Christianity), Dornach, lecture of 17 February 1923

The following table gives an overview from the year 1413 to the end of our century of how many degrees are to be subtracted depending on the respective year of birth.

year of birth	deduction	Vernal equinox	year of birth	deduction	Vernal equinox
1413	0°	0° ♈	1773	5°	25° ♓
1449	0.5°	29.5° ♓	1809	5.5°	24.5° ♓
1485	1°	29° ♓	1845	6°	24° ♓
1521	1.5°	28.5° ♓	1881	6.5°	23.5° ♓
1557	2°	28° ♓	1917	7°	23° ♓
1593	2.5°	27.5° ♓	1953	7.5°	22.5° ♓
1629	3°	27° ♓	1989	8°	22° ♓
1665	3.5°	26.5° ♓	2025	8.5°	21.5° ♓
1701	4°	26° ♓	2061	9°	21° ♓
1737	4.5°	25.5° ♓	2097	9.5°	20.5° ♓

Figure 4:
Corrections for the ephemeris from the year 1413 onwards

This is a serious fact for any amateur or professional astrologer, as all astrological charts published in books, magazines or on the Internet are based on the ephemerides. This leads to an error of several degrees in the planetary and house positions, depending on the year in which the person was born for whom the horoscope was cast. Unless, of course, the person was born at the beginning of the 15th century, when the sun actually rose at 0° ♈ at the beginning of spring. In such cases, the data from the ephemeris can be taken over unchanged. However, for people who were or will be born in the course of the 21st century, the error amounts to almost a third (!) of a zodiac sign, with a correction value of 8.5° to 9.5°.

The author is not aware of any computer program or astrological website that takes into account the precession of the vernal equinox when casting a horoscope and corrects the data from the ephemeris accordingly.

An astrological chart that has already been printed can be subsequently adapted. To do this, you must move the boundary lines between the signs of the zodiac forward (!) by the correction value given in the table above. In the astro-chart of a person born in 1989, for example, the borders of all zodiac signs should be entered at 8°, according to the correction value in the table above. A planet that was previously shown at 6° Aries in the chart is then 2° in front of the new boundary of the sign, i.e. at 28° Pisces. This then corresponds to its true position.

When creating a new astro-chart, the corresponding correction value from the above table must be subtracted from each planetary position given in the ephemeris. The Ascendant, the Medium Coeli and all other house cusps must also be moved back by the same correction value due to the retrograde shift of the vernal equinox.

Consequently, in today's common practice of astrology, the most important basis, the horoscope drawing, does not correspond to reality! It is therefore no wonder that Rudolf Steiner felt compelled to draw attention to the fact *"that almost everything that is nowadays practiced in this area is the purest dilettantism – a true superstition – and that, as far as the world at large is concerned, the true science of these things has largely been lost!"* [34]

The next chapter shows how the process of getting lost continued.

---

[34] GA 15 "Die geistige Führung des Menschen und der Menschheit" (The Spiritual Guidance of the Individual and Humanity), Copenhagen (Denmark), lecture three, 8 June 1911

The projection of the zodiac into the depths of space

Around the middle of the 16th century, Copernicus described the new heliocentric view of the world. This significantly changed the order of the planets in our solar system compared to Ptolemy's previously unchallenged geocentric view of the world. With regard to the fixed stars, however, Copernicus did not question the old doctrine of the celestial vault to which the stars were supposed to be attached. He did produce a new star catalog with partially corrected positions of the fixed stars. Otherwise, however, in his work "De Revolutionibus orbium coelestium" he merely emphasized that the sphere of the fixed stars must be extraordinarily far away from the earth. Copernicus died in 1543.

Five years later, in 1548, another revolutionary thinker was born: Giordano Bruno. His theories on the structure of creation were even more provocative than those of Copernicus. Probably the most far-reaching new idea that Giordano Bruno came up with was a real shattering of the celestial vault to his contemporaries.

At the time of Zarathustra, the founder of the primeval Persian culture, all spheres were regarded as "spiritual". They were not associated with any material concepts. The 8th sphere was the seat of the forces of the zodiac or the Cherubim, which evoked the twelve images of the zodiac in the souls of the people of early antiquity when they looked at the various directions.

In ancient Greece, when the old clairvoyance had essentially faded away, people's opinion changed to the extent that they now imagined the spheres as material hollow spheres. Their transparency and yet extraordinary stability was explained by the assumption that they were made of crystal. The earlier extrasensory and pictorial experience of the higher spiritual world as a "sea of glass, like crystal", which earned the 9th sphere the name "crystal heaven", certainly played a role here.

The 8th sphere was now imagined to be the outer end of the "visible" creation. It was assumed that all the fixed stars were attached to the inside of the 8th sphere in some way, as if to a gigantic hollow sphere. The 8th sphere thus became a rotating but nevertheless solid or "firm" celestial vault, a "Firmamentum".

Giordano Bruno clearly opposed this view, which was still prevalent even in the late Middle Ages. He claimed that there was no firmament at all, but only an infinitely deep outer space, because if infinity was a characteristic of the almighty God, then it must also be expressed in his creation. It took centuries until this completely new doctrine of Giordano Bruno finally prevailed. The heliocentric doctrine of Copernicus fared similarly. By the 19th century at the latest, the two had been combined to form the generally accepted new world view.

In astrology, this led to the zodiacal forces of the 8th sphere being transferred far out into the depths of space, because that is where all the fixed stars were now located. However, the constellations are not identical to the original extrasensory zodiacal images; they are not even coherent spatial units. The stars, which appear to be close to each other, are actually at completely different distances from the earth. There is no spatial connection at all within the so-called constellations.

The circle of zodiacal forces of our solar system is still located in the region just beyond Saturn's orbit.

At this point, let us recall some of Rudolf Steiner's statements. He explained that the zodiac consists of a circle of twelve exalted spiritual beings, the Cherubim. He then described that a planetary system is created through their interaction with the Thrones and the Seraphim, and that each planetary system becomes a new zodiac at the end of its development:

> "This is the next stage of development, that such a system, in which a sun arises from a starting point, this sun is first weak, so to speak, and has to throw out its planets so that it can develop itself further. It becomes strong, integrates its planets, becomes Vulcan. And now the whole thing dissolves, and the Vulcan sphere later becomes a hollow sphere; it then becomes something similar to this circle of the Thrones, Cherubim and Seraphim. So the sun will dissolve, sacrifice itself out into the universe, radiate its essence. And thereby it will itself become a circle of such beings as the Seraphim, Cherubim and Thrones are, which now progresses to new creation in the universe." [35]

> "An ancient solar system disappeared and faded away. Within this ancient system the ranks of the Seraphim, Cherubim, Thrones have matured to their highest degree. **Now, in accordance with the indications of the lofty Trinity, they choose a spherical space in the universe and say: here we can make a beginning.** At this moment, the Seraphim receive the aims of this new solar system, the Cherubim work them out, and the Thrones make primordial fire flow out of their own being into this spherical space." [36]

The "primordial fire" is a pure state of heat. It gradually condenses into the gaseous "primordial nebula" that science describes as the initial state of a planetary system.

---

[35] GA 110 "Geistige Hierarchien und ihre Widerspiegelung in der physischen Welt" (Spiritual Hierarchies and their Reflection in the Physical World), Düsseldorf, lecture of 14 April 1919, in the evening

[36] Ibidem

Science does not recognize the existence of spiritual entities, nor a triune God, according to whose specifications a planetary system is formed. Since the 19th century at the latest, scientists have described the universe as radically spiritless. Many of them have a clear inner feeling that there must be other living beings in the universe besides humanity. But they look for them far out in deep space and only imagine them in physical form. So today we are in the strange situation that many people imagine that absurd creatures like "E.T. the Extra-Terrestrial" or other types of "aliens" of humanoid or monster-like appearance might actually exist. But angel-like beings that are so far above humans in their development that they do not need a physical body, are regarded as unrealistic creations of fantasy.

Some cosmologists already postulate that there must be higher cosmic levels of existence, simply because the universe cannot be fully explained with all the facts known to us. But they still lack the courage to consider the possibility that these higher levels of existence are inhabited by spiritual beings who are involved in the construction of solar systems throughout the cosmos.

The following table gives an overview of the loss of knowledge of the zodiac step by step. It all began with the gradual fading of the originally clairvoyantly seen images.

The gradual loss of knowledge of the zodiac

Persia (2nd culture period)	Zodiac as the 8th sphere of our solar system	1. Clairvoyant vision of the extrasensory zodiacal images, stimulated by the forces of the twelve directions
		2. Gradual fading of the extrasensory zodiacal images
Chaldea and Babylonia (3rd culture period)		3. Determination of individual stars as physically visible boundary markers between the extrasensory zodiacal images
Greek antiquity (4th culture period)		4. Determination of twelve physically visible constellations to replace the faded extrasensory zodiacal images
		5. Fixation of the vernal equinox at 0° Aries, without taking precession into account, and compilation of an astrological set of rules, based partly on ancient transcripts, partly on abstract considerations and assumptions
Scientific age, after general acceptance of the abolition of the celestial vault by Giordano Bruno (5th culture period)	Zodiac as distant star constel- lations	6. Erroneous projection of the zodiac of our solar system onto distant constellations, i.e. onto stars that only appear to belong together, but are located at very different depths of space

Figure 5

Synopsis of the ancient world view with today's world view

In the previous chapters it was explained that the peoples of antiquity did not simply think up the spherical structure of creation, but were actually able to experience it thanks to the ancient clairvoyance that was still available at that time. According to their teachings, the zodiac is part of our solar system and is located in a region directly adjacent to the extrasensory sphere of Saturn. The latter has its sensuously perceptible image in the planet Saturn, and its orbit around the sun marks, in a sense, the outer boundary of the 7th sphere.

Beyond Saturn in our solar system is the planet Uranus and we may assume that it, like the other planets, is connected to an extrasensory sphere. According to the world view of the ancients, it would represent the 8th or zodiacal sphere. Therefore, the question arises: Is there any external evidence that relates Uranus to the zodiac and its orbit to the boundary of the area within which the extrasensory forces of the zodiac are located?

Rudolf Steiner says that Uranus is not one of the original planets of our solar system. And indeed, this planet is an eccentric with a number of characteristics that distinguish it from the other planets.

First of all, it is noticeable that it is the first of the planets that is not visible to the physical human eye in the night sky. We need a telescope to be able to see it. This is why it was only discovered towards the end of the 18th century.

Furthermore, Uranus is twice (!) as far away from the sun as Saturn. Saturn's distance from the Sun is 10 astronomical units (AU), i.e. ten times the distance between the Sun and Earth. The orbit of Uranus, however, is at a distance of 20 AU (!) from the sun. All the planets in our solar system that can be observed with the naked eye in the night sky are within 10 AU of the Sun, i.e. within Saturn's orbit. This makes Saturn the outermost member of our planetary family. The distance of Uranus, on the other hand, which is twice as great, indicates that it is only indirectly related to this family. There are no other planets within the enormous distance between the orbits of Saturn and Uranus. Uranus therefore appears to us as a completely separate element within our solar system.

The third factor is that its axis is not more or less upright, as is the case with all other planets, but is inclined by almost 90° and thus lies almost in its orbital plane. Uranus rolls on its orbit, so to speak. This also clearly distinguishes it from all other planets.

A fourth peculiarity is its orbital period. It is 84 years. This number is of particular significance as it is the product of 12 x 7. 12 is the number of the zodiac and 7 is the number of the traditional planets that it encloses.

Such peculiarities of Uranus can be interpreted as an indication that it does not belong to the planetary family of our solar system, but that its orbit marks the outer boundary of the area in which the zodiacal forces of our solar system are located, and that it is itself a representative of the 8th sphere.

According to the world view of the ancients, the 8th or zodiacal sphere is followed by a 9th sphere, the so-called "crystal heaven". Apparently there is a sensory image for this as well, because another planet orbits far beyond Uranus. It is Neptune and its orbit is just as far away from the orbit of Uranus as the latter's orbit is from the orbit of Saturn. Neptune's distance from the sun is 30 AU. Obviously there is a law in the outer region of our solar system according to which the planets orbit at intervals of 10 AU. Neptune apparently marks the outer boundary of what the ancients called the crystal heaven.

The minor planet Pluto, which is smaller than the Earth's moon, orbits the sun at an average distance of 40 AU. However, this is only the average distance of its orbit, as it has an unusually high eccentricity, so that Pluto runs within the orbit of Neptune in parts. Pluto's distance from the Sun varies between 29.7 AU (approx. 30 AU) and 49.3 AU (approx. 50 AU).

Astronomers refer to the area beyond Neptune's orbit, in which Pluto moves, as the "Kuiper Belt", after the Dutch-born US astronomer Gerard Peter Kuiper. An enormous number of small celestial bodies orbit in this distant region of our solar system. According to the ancient world view, this is the sphere of the "Primum Mobile", the First Mover. Even though natural science does not seriously consider the existence of spiritual entities which were related to these regions far outside the seven planetary spheres by the ancients, the structure of our solar system based on clairvoyant perception is in line with the latest research findings. Even beyond Saturn's orbit there are regions or spheres whose boundaries are indicated by the orbit of a planet.

Until now, it was assumed that the Kuiper Belt extends to a distance of 50 AU from the Sun, i.e. exactly as far as the maximum distance of Pluto's orbit. In the meantime, however, the space probe New Horizons has reached a distance of almost 60 AU and measured a dust density there that was unexpectedly high to the researchers, so that there is currently a debate as to whether the Kuiper Belt extends to this distance or even further.

The "solar wind", a stream of charged particles emanating from our Sun, is effective in regions even beyond the Kuiper belt. Its area of effect is referred to as the "heliosphere". Contrary to the generally accepted idea of extremely cold space with a temperature of around -455 °F (-270 °C), the Voyager 2 space probe, launched in 1977, measured temperatures of +11,000 K (19,340 °F) in the outer region of our solar system, beyond the Kuiper belt. And when, at a distance of around 94 AU from our Sun, the probe crossed the so-called "termination shock" of our heliosphere, the zone where the solar wind collides with the interstellar medium and is dammed up by it, the measurements even showed a sudden rise in temperature to +180,000 K (323,540 °F). This was about 30 AU beyond the Kuiper Belt. Is this a physical expression of what the ancients called the "Empyrean", the "fire heaven"? In any case, the probe's measurements prove the existence of a gigantic thermal envelope surrounding our solar system, similar to the way the thermosphere or ionosphere envelops the Earth.

Another 30 AU further out in space, i.e. at a distance of around 124 AU from the sun, is the outer boundary of the heliosphere, the so-called heliopause. Beyond the Kuiper Belt, the distances between the spheres therefore appear to be 30 AU. Saturn's distance from the sun, which is "only" 10 AU, would fit three times into such a huge distance. So, if we just count the planets up to Saturn as belonging to our actual planetary system, then this would have a diameter of 20 AU. This means that our planetary system, bounded by Saturn, would fit one and a half times between the boundaries of two of the outer spheres of our solar system. This may give us an idea of the gigantic dimensions of these outer spheres.

In April 2024, Voyager 2 traveled to a distance of 136 AU (!) from the Sun and thus, according to today's definition, into interstellar space.

Our solar system is therefore not only divided into the planetary area and its spheres, but also into a transplanetary area in which Uranus, Neptune and Pluto orbit. And the peripheral zone of the solar system is divided into further spheres as well. The dimensions of the spheres and the distances between their boundaries increase the further they extend into space.

The peoples of antiquity had teachings that referred to such distant spheres. They described the existence of 7 worlds or planes of existence. According to their teaching, the spheres of our solar system only extend over the three lowest planes: the physical world, the soul world, also known as the astral plan, and the spirit world or the mental plan. But, there are four further, trans-spiritual worlds above these: the Bud(d)hi Plane, the Atma or Nirvana Plane, then the Paranirvana Plane and finally, as the seventh, the Mahaparanirvana Plane. These four highest, trans-spiritual worlds have their sensuous image in the stellar and galactic realms. Above all reigns the threefold Logos, the supreme triune deity, who, in the creation and development of the universe, makes use of a multitude of spiritual beings of the most varied ranks, all of which once emerged from Him.

According to the teachings of the ancients, each of the 7 worlds consists of 7 spheres. However, the worlds overlap in such a way that the three upper spheres of one world penetrate the three lower spheres of the next higher world.

The following figure provides an overview of the cosmic planes and also shows a synopsis of the ancient world view with today's world view.

Ancient world view | The threefold Logos | Modern world view

Images of the extrasensory planes of existence in the physical world

Ancient world view			The threefold Logos	Modern world view
Higher Paranirvana plane	galactic	Higher Mahaparanirvana plane		entire universe
Lower Paranirvana plane	spheres	Lower Mahaparanirvana plane		galaxy clusters
Higher Budhi plane	starry	Higher Atma plane		galaxies
Lower Budhi plane	spheres	Lower Atma plane		star clusters
Higher astral plane	4. Sun Sphere / 3. Venus Sphere / 2. Mercury Sphere	Higher mental plane	11. Empyrean / 10. Primum Mobile / 9. Crystal heaven / 8. Zodiacal Sphere / 7. Saturn Sphere / 6. Jupiter Sphere / 5. Mars Sphere	Heliosphere / Kuiper belt / Neptune Sphere / Uranus Sphere — our solar system
Lower astral plane	1. Moon Sphere	Lower mental plane		
		Higher physical plane	Life ether / Chem. ether / Light ether / Fire (ether)	terrestrial area
		Lower physical plane	Air / Water / Earth	

Figure 6: Synopsis of the ancient world view with today's world view

Skeptics may take offense at the fact that the number 7 plays such a large role here. Sometimes this is seen as a naïve preference of ancient peoples for abstruse number mysticism. However, the same accusation should be made against modern science, as it teaches us that the periodic table of the elements consists of 7 main groups, that the light spectrum shows 7 colors and that the harmony of music is based on 7 notes, because the 8th note, the octave, is the first note of the next higher series of seven. It is not for nothing that 7 has always been considered a "sacred number".

Under the influence of today's prevailing materialism, our scientists limit their view to the physical world. They only look broadly, as it were, trying to understand the world as a whole with a purely "horizontal world view". They still do not dare to look up to higher dimensions and seriously consider them.

Admittedly, the peoples of prehistoric times had far less detailed knowledge of the physical world than we do today. Instead, however, they cultivated a "vertical world view" that included higher planes of existence and the beings that inhabit them. They had a detailed knowledge about this that we completely lack today.

When looking at the synopsis of the ancient and the new world view in Figure 6, are we not encouraged to drop any arrogance that labels the ancients as superstitious fantasists? They possessed truly astonishing knowledge. We should therefore rather wonder whether those people who merely cultivate a spiritless, purely materialistic and substance-based view of the world are not much more likely to be superstitious fantasists.

According to our cosmologists, the entire universe is said to have been created by a gigantic explosion, the so-called Big Bang. However, researchers do not know what the universe as a whole really consists of. They speculate that there is dark matter and dark energy, as the structure of the universe cannot really be explained with all the components known to date. This theory is now being called into question. Nevertheless, some researchers claim that they can say exactly which elementary particles were formed in the first billionth of a second (!) after the Big Bang. And then the entire universe with all the laws of nature and the unbelievably gigantic amount of matter in it came into being quite automatically.

All the wisdom in the structure of the universe, even the incomprehensible wisdom that we can observe in all things here on earth, in the growth, blossoming, fruiting and ripening of the plant world, in the reproductive processes, in the diverse life of the animal kingdom and even in the cultural development of humanity, all of this simply came about in this way? The phenomena of life and consciousness, which are in quality so completely different from matter, are merely by-products of matter? Isn't that extremely naïve? Shouldn't it rather be called an unrealistic fantasy and therefore superstition?

The ancient peoples experienced and saw with their ancient clairvoyance how higher beings are at work everywhere in nature, wisely forming and directing. If they had been told about the ideas of our proud modern natural science, which seem pathetic in comparison, they would certainly have looked with great regret and pity at them.

Rudolf Steiner announced that the spiritless world view of today's humanity will only be a transitional phase. In the future, people's perception will once again extend into extrasensory regions. New fields of research will then be discovered and natural science, which is only interested in matter, will be supplemented by a science of the higher planes of existence and their inhabitants. In this way, humanity will advance towards a true spiritual science. It is the task of anthroposophy to lay the foundations for this today.

The lost knowledge of the house system

The previous considerations referred to the planets and the zodiac. They are the two most important basic elements of astrology. However, there is a third one. This is the so-called "house system". Much of the original knowledge about this has also been lost. Today's astrology no longer has any authentic knowledge about it.

The house system is based on the law that not only the year is divided into 12 months, but also the day into 12 double hours of different qualities that are connected to the 12 forces of the zodiac. The early morning was regarded as the first double hour and accordingly the region of the sunrise, i.e. the east, was called the first house or first field.

The vast majority of astrological schools define the first house as beginning directly at the rising point in the East, the Ascendant. They attribute to it and the double hour immediately preceding the characteristics of the zodiacal image of Aries. This is based on the late antique tradition of assigning both the Ascendant as the rising point in the daily cycle and the vernal point in the annual cycle to 0° ♈. Some astrologers take a different view. They place the Ascendant as the "cusp" of the first house in the center of this house, i.e. at 15° ♈. Similarly, they regard the "cusps" of the other eleven houses as the middle of the house. Nevertheless, there is general agreement that the characteristics of the houses correspond exactly to the order of the zodiac.

However, there is no agreement on the size of the individual houses. There are house systems with houses of equal size and those with houses of unequal size. But the unequally sized houses are very different in size, depending on the school. Over the centuries, a whole range of different "house systems" have emerged in this way. There is, for example, one according to Placidus, but also one according to Koch, Campanus, Regiomontanus and others.

Unfortunately, the assignment of the first house to Aries is based on a rigidly inherited tradition from ancient Greece. At that time it was true. Today it no longer corresponds to reality. The counter-clockwise counting of the houses is also wrong. It probably arose because the series of zodiac signs in the astrological chart runs counterclockwise. This order was simply transferred to the houses.

Rudolf Steiner's accusation that "dilettantism" and "superstition" prevail in today's astrology therefore also applies to the common concept of the house system.

But is there any way to get back to the original teaching of the houses? – There is indeed one. The first thing to remember is that the ascendant corresponds to the east. It is the "rising point", in particular the point of sunrise. When the ancients spoke of the cardinal point east, they usually used the term "towards sunrise". When they spoke of the south, they simply said "towards noon". Correspondingly, the west was "towards sunset" and the north "towards midnight". This shows how much importance was attached to the Sun and its movement in the sky during the course of the day, as well as the relationship of this movement to the four cardinal points.

We find this expressed in the illustration of the ancient world view in Schedel's World Chronicle of 1493, where, in addition to the spheres, the winds of the four cardinal points are depicted in the form of human heads and given names (see Figure 1, page 27). In astrology, a reminder of this has been preserved at least to the extent that the four corners of the house system are given special significance. The ascendant corresponds to the east, the medium coeli (midheaven) to the south, the descendant to the west and the imum coeli (lowest heaven) to the north.

Although all four points of the compass played a major role for the ancient peoples, a particularly prominent position was always assigned to the east as the "sunrise point". This fact will be examined in more detail below in order to gain a better understanding of the house system.

The importance of the point of sunrise for the development of mankind

In the previous chapters, we have already discussed the great influence of the slow backward shift of the vernal equinox through the zodiac on the cultural development of humanity. Accordingly, Rudolf Steiner calls the ancient primeval Persian culture, during which the Sun rose at the beginning of spring in the area of the zodiacal image of Gemini, the "Age of Gemini". The subsequent Egyptian-Chaldean-Babylonian epoch is also called the "Age of Taurus", because at that time the point of sunrise at the beginning of spring was for 2,160 years in the direction from which forces flowed onto the earth, which evoked the image of a bull-like animal in people's souls when they looked there.

This perception had a decisive influence on the culture and religious cult of the time. The priests knew that the extrasensory image of a bull was an expression of a high spiritual being. The earthly animal, the bull, was only the visible symbol of this. Therefore, the sacred bull Apis was worshipped in Egypt at that time. It carried a sun disk between its horns as a sign of his affiliation to the sunrise. It also represented the life force in nature. In addition, the ancient Egyptian priests knew that at the time of sunrise in the east at the beginning of spring, in the exact opposite direction, in the west, the point of sunset was in the zodiacal image of Scorpio. It represents death and the afterlife in the higher worlds.

Since the ancient Egyptians still had memories of an existence before birth and were also able to follow their deceased relatives part of the way through the spheres of the higher worlds with the remains of their innate clairvoyance, they understood "life" to mean not only life on earth, as is the case with us today, but to them there was a life after birth on earth and a life after death in the spiritual world. Both were ruled by high spiritual beings. Life on earth in this world was governed by the divine being Isis, the patron goddess of birth. Life in the afterlife in the higher worlds was ruled by her brother and husband Osiris, the patron god of death. And since the moon governs the cycle of fertility of earthly bodies on the one hand, but is also the ruler of the night sky on the other, the Isis-Osiris cult was a moon cult. It was at this time that lunar religions emerged among the peoples of the Near East.

But it was not only the sunrise at the beginning of spring and the beginning of autumn that shaped Egyptian cult and culture. The summer and winter solstices also played a prominent role back then. The solstices always follow the equinoxes at intervals of a quarter of a year. They therefore shift together with the vernal equinox and the autumnal equinox due to the slow rotation of the Earth's axis. Today we associate the winter solstice with 0° Capricorn. At least that's what the ephemerides say. However, this information must be corrected as shown in the table on page 53.

At the time of the ancient Egyptians, when the vernal equinox was in Taurus and the autumnal equinox in Scorpio, the Sun rose at the winter solstice in the area of the zodiacal image of Aquarius and at the summer solstice in the area of the zodiacal image of Leo. This is why the Taurus-Scorpio and Leo-Aquarius axes were considered the two main axes of the year.

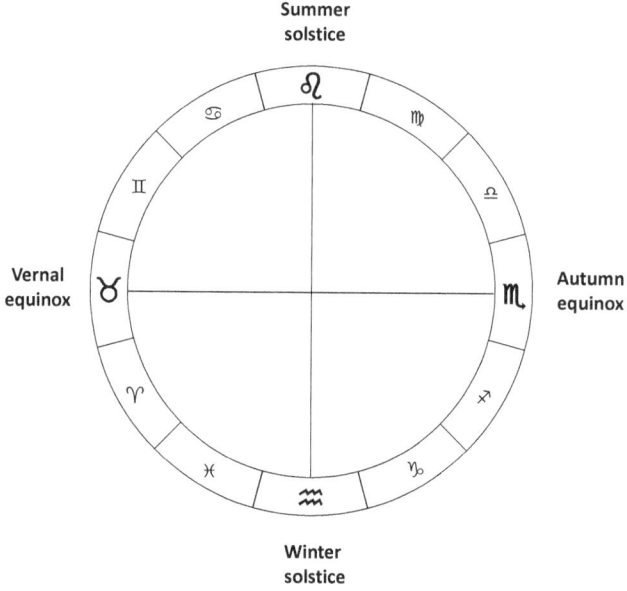

Figure 7:
The two main axes of the year
in the Age of Taurus

The most important religious celebrations were held on the days near the summer and winter solstices. These were highly spiritual feasts, because during these days the Isis priestess could seek the advice of the gods. As a result of her special preparation in the Egyptian mysteries, she was able to read the aura of the Sun.[37] In this way she learned what special precautions needed to be taken for the next half of the year.

Rudolf Steiner told us about the Isis priestess's reading in the solar aura:

"And the priests tried to detect from the statements of the Isis priestess, from what she found in the solar aura, and wrote down: Rainy year, sowing the seeds at a certain time – in short, all practical things that were important for the guidance of life in the following year. They lived according to these directions because they knew how the heavens work down onto the earth." [38]

Due to the extraordinary importance of the solstice celebrations under the influence of the zodiacal images of Leo and Aquarius, the ancient Egyptians created a huge sculpture at the beginning of the Age of Taurus, which was intended to express the significance of the Leo-Aquarius axis in the course of the year. It is the famous Sphinx of Giza. It consists of a lion's body with a human head, because the zodiacal image that we call Aquarius today was once seen as a human

---

[37] According to Rudolf Steiner, the Isis priestess was only able to read the sun's aura because the earth crosses the sun's path twice a year. The Sun leaves an impression in the ether on its path. From a Copernican perspective, a crossing of the two paths is not possible. According to Rudolf Steiner, however, the planets and the Sun move along lemniscatory paths and cross at their center twice a year. A detailed discussion of this topic can be found in the author's book "The Lemniscatory Path System", published by BoD (Books on Demand), Norderstedt (Germany).

[38] GA 171 "Innere Entwicklungsimpulse der Menschheit. Goethe und die Krisis des 19. Jahrhunderts" (Inner Impulses of Human Evolution – Goethe and the Crisis of the 19th Century), lecture of 1 October 1916

head. This is also how the evangelist John described it in chapter 4:7 of his Revelation.

In order to unmistakably connect the Leo-Aquarius sculpture of the Sphinx with the sunrise point, it was created in a west-east direction. The Sphinx faces east, where the sun rises above the horizon early in the morning on the winter solstice in the image of Aquarius.

To the ancient Egyptians, the earthly representative of the divine cosmic forces of this main axis of the year was the pharaoh. It was therefore decided to transform the initially impersonal face of the sphinx into the face of the reigning pharaoh. This procedure was maintained by some of the early, successive pharaohs. For this purpose, the head of the sphinx had to be adjusted after each new accession to the throne and a little more material had to be chiseled off the stone mass of the head. In the end, it became so disproportionately small compared to the giant lion's body that this procedure was abandoned.

We can see from all these things how extremely important the connection between the sunrise at the key points of the year and the zodiacal forces revealing in extrasensory images was to people at these times.

The importance of the point of sunrise for the house system

As already mentioned, not only the year but also the day was divided by the ancients according to the number 12, subdividing it into 12 double hours, not 24 hours as we do today. They knew that not only the course of the year was subject to the twelve high entities of the zodiac, but also the course of the day.

The light half of the day corresponds to the light half of the year and the night half of the day corresponds to the dark half of the year. Similarly, the beginning of spring corresponds to the sunrise in the east every morning, the summer solstice to the daily highest point of the sun at noon in the south, the beginning of fall to the sunset in the west and the winter solstice to the lowest point of the sun at midnight in the north. In the horoscope, these four corner points are referred to as the Ascendant = rising point in the east, Medium Coeli = midheaven in the south, Descendant = descending point in the west and Imum Coeli = depth of the sky in the north. Therefore, their positions in one of the zodiacal images and the planets that are close to them at the time of a person's birth are of the greatest importance, especially the Ascendant as the rising point in the east.

The special characteristics that the rising point in the east receives from the zodiacal force in whose area the sun rises at the beginning of spring also characterize the *daily* sunrise point for the duration of an entire age. For this reason, in the Age of Taurus, the ascendant was closely linked to the properties of the zodiacal image of Taurus. Its forces essentially had an effect in the first house of the horoscope.

In the following Age of Aries, at the time of Ptolemy, both the vernal equinox as the annual rising point of the sun in the east and the Ascendant as the daily rising point were under the influence of the extrasensory image of Aries. Accordingly, the ancient Greeks associated the first house with the qualities of Aries. This assignment was retained by most astrologers over the following two thousand years. Many other rules from that time were also simply adopted. They were and are still applied almost dogmatically today, although most of them were only established in times when ancient clairvoyance had long since faded away. As a result, many of these rules are little related to reality.

As far as the Ascendant is concerned, another deviation from reality is the practice among astrologers of completely ignoring the shift of the vernal equinox. In all ephemerides, the position of the Sun at the beginning of spring on March 22/23 is given as 0° ♈. And since the month of Aries is the first month of the year, the first house of the horoscope is also strictly assigned to Aries.

One may wonder why Ptolemy, who describes in the Almagest his assumption that the vernal equinox shifts by 1 degree in the zodiac every 100 years, did not include this in his astrological work Tetrabiblos. Perhaps he wrote it before the Almagest. Irrespective of this, the Tetrabiblos appears to be simply a collection of all the astrological rules that could somehow be learned at the time, similar to the way the Brothers Grimm collected and wrote down the fairy tales passed down orally in the 19th century. And the shift of the vernal equinox assumed by Ptolemy by just 1° every 100 years had no significance for his contemporaries anyway. It would only have come into effect over the next few centuries.

Today the vernal equinox is at 21.5° ♓. This means that the Ascendant in the horoscope of a person born in our time is also at 21.5° ♓. The influence of Pisces begins 8.5° above the Ascendant and ends 21.5° below it. We can therefore conclude that:

1. The characteristics of the first house and its cusp, the Ascendant, change from age to age. During the time of the ancient Egyptians, in the Age of Taurus, the first house and the Ascendant showed characteristics of the zodiacal image of Taurus. In the subsequent Age of Aries, during the Greco-Roman cultural epoch,

the influence of Aries prevailed in the same area of the horoscope. In today's Piscean Age, the forces of the zodiacal image of Pisces are at work there.

2. The rule applied by some astrologers, according to which planets that are a few degrees above the Ascendant are to be attributed to the same and to the first house, is quite correct today. The zodiacal force that rules the first house and the Ascendant has an effect of up to 8.5° in the area above the Ascendant in our time. Around the year 2500, the Ascendant will even be in the middle of the zodiacal image of Pisces. Then the rule used by other astrologers will apply, according to which the house cusps are always to be evaluated as the middle of a house. In our century, this rule is premature.

3. What applies to the Ascendant also applies to all other house cusps. In the first half of our century, these also are at 8.5° of the respective zodiacal image. For people of earlier centuries, the respective correction value can be found in the table on page 53.

4. The order of the houses runs clockwise! Only the order of the signs of the zodiac runs counter-clockwise, not the order of the houses, because the sun moves from east to south during the course of the day, sets in the west and passes through the north at midnight. In the horoscope, this corresponds to the sequence of Ascendant, Medium Coeli, Descendant, Imum Coeli, and thus clockwise. All houses should therefore be drawn in exactly the opposite direction to that taught by almost all schools of astrology or astrosophy today.

The latter has the consequence that pretty much all interpretations that refer to planetary positions in the houses are completely beyond reality. They are interpretations based on a false foundation. Again, we see how justified Rudolf Steiner's judgement was when he described today's astrology as essentially "dilettantism" and "superstition".

At this point, the question may arise as to whether Rudolf Steiner himself gave a description of the house system. He did indeed comment on it in a lecture on the future turn of science towards the forces of the cosmos.

The future turn of science towards the forces of the cosmos

In 1917 Rudolf Steiner gave a lecture with some surprising statements on the further development of science in the Age of the Consciousness Soul or the Piscean Age, which will last until the middle of the 4th millennium AD:

*"In the future there will be a great battle. Human science will stretch out to the cosmic, but will try to get there by different paths. It will be the task of good, healing science to find certain cosmic forces which can reach the earth through the co-operation of two cosmic streams, those of **Pisces** and **Virgo**. The great secret to be discovered will be how the influence which works from the direction of Pisces as a power of the sun unites itself with the influence working from the direction of Virgo. It will make for good when it is learnt how the **morning and evening forces** from two sides of the cosmos can be brought into the service of humanity; on one side from the part of **Pisces**, on the other from the part of **Virgo**."* [39]

---

[39] GA 178 "Individuelle Geistwesen und ihr Wirken in der Seele des Menschen" (Individual Spirit Beings and their Activity in the Human Soul), Dornach, lecture of 25 November 1917

In addition to these words, Rudolf Steiner drew a sketch on the blackboard regarding the effectiveness of the zodiacal forces in the course of the day (!) and thus the connection between the zodiacal forces and the houses that is valid in our age. Because of the great importance of his further explanations, they are reproduced below in full.

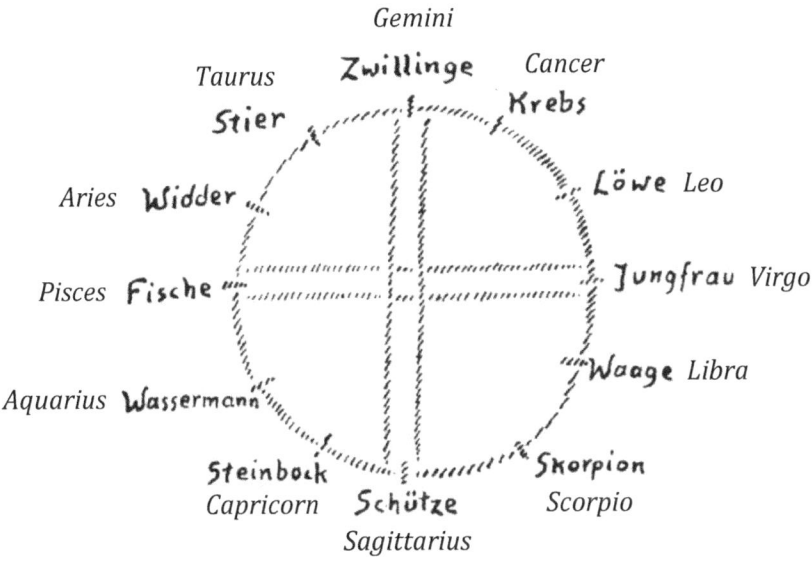

Figure 8:
**Rudolf Steiner's sketch
on the effectiveness of the forces of the zodiac
during the course of the day**

"These forces, however, will be left aside by those who try to achieve their whole purpose through the dualism of polarity, by positive and negative forces. The spiritual secrets which on earth – with the help of the dual forces of magnetism, the positive and negative – can allow the spiritual to be penetrated by the cosmic, come from the **Gemini** *in the*

universe; they are the **midday forces**. In ancient times already it was known that cosmic influences were involved in this, and today even exoteric scientists are aware that in some or other way positive and negative magnetism lie behind **Gemini** in the Zodiac. One will strive to paralyse all that could be gained through a revelation of the duality in the cosmos – to paralyse it in a materialistic, egotistic way by means of the forces which stream to humanity particularly from **Gemini** and can be placed entirely at the service of the human 'Double'.

Other [occult] brotherhoods, concerned above all to divert attention from the Mystery of Golgotha, will try to make use of the duality in human nature – the duality which, just as man has moved into the fifth post-Atlantean epoch, comprises the human being, but within him the lower animal nature. A human being is really a centaur in a certain sense: he contains the lower animal nature in its astral form, he contains the human, so to speak, only added on top of this animal nature. The working together of this duality in man gives rise to a duality of forces as well. This duality of forces will be utilised particularly by certain egotistic brotherhoods, chiefly from the side of India and the East, in order to mislead eastern Europe, whose task it is to prepare for the sixth post-Atlantean epoch. And this will be done with the aid of the forces which work in from **Sagittarius**.

The conquest of the cosmic for humanity in a twofold incorrect way or in a single correct way, that is what awaits humanity. **This will bring about a real renewal for astrology, which in its old form was atavistic and cannot continue to exist in this old form.**

Those who know about the cosmos will fight each other; one side will apply the **morning and evening processes** in the way I have indicated; the West will use the **midday processes**, shutting out the morning and evening ones; and the East will use the **midnight**

processes. Men will no longer manufacture substances on the basis merely of chemical attraction and repulsion; they will know that different substances arise according to whether they are made with morning and evening processes, or with midday or midnight ones. It will be known that such substances act in a quite different way on the triad, God, virtue and immortality – gold, health and prolongation of life.

Nothing wrong can be achieved through the interaction of what comes from **Pisces and Virgo**. One will achieve something through which the mechanism of life will be detached, in a certain sense, from man himself, but will not give any group power and rulership over another. The cosmic forces drawn from this side will create remarkable machines, but only those that will relieve man of work, because they will carry a certain power of intelligence within themselves. And a Spiritual Science which itself reaches out towards the cosmic will have to see to it that all the great temptations which come from these machine-animals, created by man himself, are not allowed to exercise any harmful influence upon him."

Rudolf Steiner's words, spoken at the beginning of the 20th century, could hardly have described the robots of the current 21st century more aptly. He calls them "machine-animals" and points out that they are not only to be seen in a negative light, but can and will be used in a positive sense for humanity. Ahrimanic letterpress printing can also be used for positive purposes, as we can see from the book publications of Rudolf Steiner's lectures. He was never concerned with a general demonization of technology. He repeatedly emphasized that it is part of human development. Humanity must also go through a technical phase. It is just a matter of using things in the right way, for the good of mankind, without falling prey to the temptations towards the negative that are also associated with technology.

In any case, in Rudolf Steiner's sketch we have a clear representation of the house system with an assignment of the zodiacal forces to the 12 double hours of the day in a clockwise direction. And the way in which he positioned the zodiacal images of Gemini and Sagittarius at the top and bottom exactly in the middle, and also the zodiacal images of Pisces and Virgo exactly on the horizontal axis of the figure, shows that his sketch refers to our Piscean age as a whole. He has depicted the situation as it will occur in the middle of the age. By then the vernal equinox will have moved back exactly to the center of Pisces, and the Ascendant will also be exactly at 15° Pisces in the house system as the east point of the horoscope. This will be the case around the year 2500, because if we add half the duration of 2,160 years, i.e. 1080 years, to the beginning of our age in the year 1413, we get the year 2493.

In about 100 years, the first third of the Piscean Age will have ended and the middle period will begin. However, even today we can clearly see the increasing interest of researchers in magnetism and its use for practical purposes.

It may now be interesting to ask whether Rudolf Steiner applied the effectiveness of the zodiacal forces in the course of the day, as he himself described it, in any practical way. He actually did so, in connection with an extremely important event, namely the setting of the date for the laying of the foundation stone for the first Goetheanum.

The date of the laying of the foundation stone for the first Goetheanum

The construction of the first Goetheanum in Dornach was a major challenge to the Anthroposophical Society. The building was primarily conceived as a worthy setting for the performance of the Mystery Dramas written by Rudolf Steiner and, with its completely new architectural style, the design of the stained glass windows, columns, architraves and ceiling paintings, it was intended to be an awesome expression of the spiritual world view of anthroposophy. The couple Dr. Oskar Grosheintz and Mrs. Nelly Grosheintz-Laval kindly made the front part of the building site available for the Goetheanum. The rear part had to be purchased.

Rudolf Steiner had a foundation stone crafted that consisted of a double dodecahedron with two unequal halves made of copper and a pyrite hanging in the middle of each half. Pyrite is an iron sulphide, a compound of the Mars metal iron with sulphur ($FeS2$). This compound was probably chosen by Rudolf Steiner in order to counterbalance the Venus metal copper and thus bring the foundation stone into equilibrium.

For the laying of the foundation stone a pit was prepared and concreted, into which seven steps led down. In the evening, the double dodecahedron was placed there in a west-east direction, in such a way that the large dodecahedron lay to the east and the small dodecahedron to the west, exactly the opposite of the later small dome of the Goetheanum to the east and the large dome to the west.

Initially, Rudolf Steiner kept the date he had planned for the laying of the foundation stone a secret. His close associates only knew that the date would be announced at very short notice, and therefore only a small group of people would be able to attend. Mrs. Nelly Grosheintz-Laval later reported that Rudolf Steiner had announced the date of September 20 as the day of the laying of the foundation stone only three days beforehand.[40]

In the afternoon of that day, he created a document on a bull's skin that was prepared especially for this purpose. He drew a large egg shape and within this form a sketch of the double dodecahedron, surrounded by initial letters referring to the Trinity and the nine angelic hierarchies. In addition to other notes, Rudolf Steiner wrote in conclusion:

GELEGT VOM J.B.V. FÜR DIE ANTHROPOSOPHISCHE ARBEIT
AM 20ten TAGE DES SEPTEMBER MONATS 1880 n. d. M. v. G.
d. i. 1913 n. CH. GEB. DA ♀ ALS ABENDSTERN IN DER WAAGE STAND

Laid by J.B.V. for the anthroposophical work
on the 20th day of the month of September 1880 a. th. M. o. G.
i.e. 1913 AD when ♀ as the evening star was in Libra.

"J.B.V" is the abbreviation of "Johannesbauverein", which means (St.) John Building's Association. This association was responsible for the construction of the building and was founded specifically for this purpose, as the "Goetheanum" was originally to be built in Munich under the name "Johannesbau".

"n. d. M. v. G." (in English: a. th. M. o. G.) means "nach dem Mysterium von Golgatha" (after the Mystery of Golgatha). According to Rudolf Steiner, the Mystery of Golgatha took place in 33 AD.

---

[40] See the eyewitness reports by Nelly Grosheintz-Laval and Max Benzinger in "Erinnerungen an Rudolf Steiner" (Memories of Rudolf Steiner), edited by Erika Beltle and Kurt Vierl, publisher Freies Geistesleben, Germany (3rd edition 2017)

Calculated from this year, the year 1913 corresponds to the year 1880. In this sense, the laying of the foundation stone took place in September 1880 a. th. M. o. G.

The document was inserted into the double dodecahedron, which was then soldered with tin. The bull skin of the document was probably intended to make a further contribution to the balance of forces in the foundation stone.

Rudolf Steiner's aim was quite obviously to create a state of equilibrium, and the timing of the laying of the foundation stone was chosen accordingly. Strangely enough, however, the date he chose was three days before the beginning of autumn. In 1913, this was on September 23, shortly before 6 pm. The question therefore arises as to why Rudolf Steiner did not wait the few days until the autumnal equinox.

Apparently it was important to him that "Mercury, as the evening star, was in Libra", as he himself noted on the document. But was Mercury really in Libra on September 20, 1913, when the foundation stone was laid? According to the ephemeris, it had only just crossed the border between Virgo and Libra at around 11 a.m. that day. The ceremony was scheduled to begin at 6.30 pm. At this time, Mercury had only moved half a degree into Libra! It was therefore still in the transitional area between the two signs. Rudolf Steiner's explicit formulation in the document of the foundation stone therefore seems rather "borderline". If he considered the connection between Mercury and Libra to be so important, why didn't he simply wait the three days until the autumnal equinox? Then Mercury would have reached at least 5° Libra.

One could argue that the foundation stone was laid at sunset and that Mercury, as the evening star, was therefore on the Descendant, which according to the rules of traditional astrology is the cusp of the 7th house or the house of Libra. However, this house is located above the Descendant and not below it. But the foundation stone was laid *after* sunset.

Apart from the houses, the situation could also be interpreted to mean that Mercury was in balance between the day and night half around sunset. This would have placed it in "equilibrium" (Libra), at least in a figurative sense.

However, contrary to the original plan, the ceremony only began at 7 p.m. and lasted an hour and a half. The site even had to be illuminated by a pile of wood that had been specially prepared and set on fire. Thus, it was already dark when the ceremony took place and Mercury had already sunk far below the horizon. According to traditional astrology, Mercury passed through the houses of Virgo and Leo for the duration of the ceremony.

There is even another point of view that suggests that Mercury was in Virgo at the time the foundation stone was laid and not in Libra, yet not with regard to the house but with regard to the zodiac. According to Rudolf Steiner's indications, all planetary positions in the ephemeris of the year 1913 must be corrected by subtracting 7° in each case in order to take account of the retrograde shift of the vernal equinox, as shown in the table on page 53. Consequently, on September 20, Mercury was not in 0.5° Libra as the ephemeris indicates, but 7° before it. That means it was in 23.5° Virgo! Even three days later, at the autumnal equinox, Mercury would only have reached 28° Virgo and not 5° Libra. This makes the wording in the foundation stone document even more questionable.

Rudolf Steiner's thoughts regarding the scheduling of the great event were obviously completely different from what is generally assumed. On closer inspection, however, it is precisely the consideration of the precession of the vernal equinox that leads to the solution of the problem.

As can be seen from the table on page 53 with the correction values for the precession of the vernal equinox, in 1913 it was located at 23° Pisces. In the previous chapters, the great importance of the shift of the vernal equinox through the zodiac with regard to the cultural development of mankind was already explained. Of equal importance is the accompanying shift of the autumn point, which is located directly opposite the vernal point in the zodiac. Thus, in 1913 it was at 23° Virgo. And this is exactly where Mercury was on September 20, 1913! This is not the point of the annual beginning of autumn, but instead, around 1913 it was the autumn point in terms of the Age, which is much more significant. We can see from this that Rudolf Steiner considered the laying of the foundation stone for the first Goetheanum to be an event of cultural importance for the entire Piscean Age. Now we can appreciate it in a completely new way.

However, the question still remains as to why Rudolf Steiner so explicitly noted on the foundation stone deed that "Mercury, as the evening star, was in Libra". An answer to this question can only be found if one considers his statements and his sketch of the effectiveness of the zodiacal forces during the course of the day, as shown in Figure 8 on page 79. There you can see the clockwise house system according to Rudolf Steiner. It differs fundamentally from the abstractly thought up house systems of traditional astrology, which run counter-clockwise.

This results in the following situation for the time when the foundation stone was laid: On September 20, 1913 at 7 p.m., when the ceremonial act began, Mercury had already sunk 13° below the horizon. According to Rudolf Steiner's house system, the Descendant was at 23° Virgo in 1913. Consequently, the first 7 degrees of the 13 degrees below the Descendant were still under Virgo's influence and the following 6 degrees were in the house of Libra (see Figure 9). Consequently, at 7 pm, Mercury had arrived at 6° in the house of Libra. At 8.30 pm, at the end of the laying of the foundation stone, Mercury had reached the position of 52° below the horizon due to the rotation of the Earth. It was now in the middle of the house of Scorpio. However, this means nothing other than that Mercury was in the house of Libra for most of the time during the ceremonial laying of the foundation stone, which lasted an hour and a half.

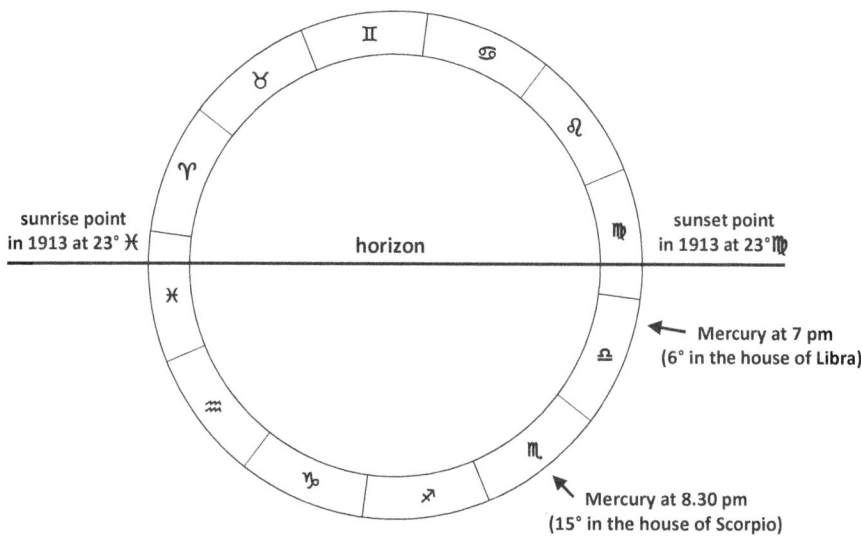

Figure 9:
The positions of Mercury on the evening
of the laying of the foundation stone for the first Goetheanum,
according to Rudolf Steiner's house system

Thus, Rudolf Steiner was quite right to note on the document incorporated into the double dodecahedron regarding the ceremonial act of laying the foundation stone: "when ☿ as the evening star was in Libra." Even if the laying act had begun at 6.30 p.m., as originally planned, this statement would have been correct. The time he chose for the act of laying the foundation stone for the first Goetheanum according to cosmic aspects is therefore in full harmony with his statements on the significance of the vernal equinox for the individual ages and on the effectiveness of the forces of the zodiac during the course of the day.

Epilog

From the example of Rudolf Steiner laying the foundation stone for the first Goetheanum, we can see how important it is to take into account the precession of the vernal equinox both for the exact determination of planetary positions in the zodiac and in the house system. His harsh criticism of astrology was not directed against it in general, but against its teachings, which had gradually fallen into disrepair over the millennia. This also includes the erroneous identification of the zodiac of our solar system with distant star constellations, which had already occurred in ancient Greece. These are not even spatially coherent units. Viewed from Earth, their stars appear to be next to each other. In reality, however, they are located at completely different depths in space. They actually have no spatial connection with each other.

The night sky is only the background against which the zodiac of our solar system, *invisible* to the physical eye, is located. Our planetary system once emerged from this and will develop into such a circle of forces, just like every other planetary system in the great universe.

On top of all this, the knowledge of the house system was turned into the opposite by reversing the direction from "clockwise" to "counter-clockwise".

Over the millennia, the elementary foundations of astrology were actually distorted to such an extent that it was soon no longer possible to draw a correct astrological chart, which is the absolutely necessary basis for a subsequent interpretation.

The extensive rules of interpretation are also mainly based on ancient traditions, into which more and more fantasy and superstition have crept. Nevertheless, many astrologers apply them almost dogmatically. Of course, there is no denying that there have always been accurate astrological forecasts. For example, the Danish astronomer and astrologer Tycho Brahe (1546 - 1601) predicted at the age of 20 the death of sultan Suleiman, which actually happened, albeit not exactly on the predicted date. However, the number of unfulfilled astrological prophecies is many times greater than those that actually came true. We humans tend to remember what has come true and suppress the false predictions. Tycho Brahe's astrological predictions may have been helped by the fact that during his lifetime in the 16th century, the vernal equinox had only moved back 2° from 0° ♈ into Pisces and was at 28° ♓. The planetary positions calculated by Brahe therefore still corresponded approximately to their actual position in the extrasensory zodiac. Nevertheless, there were countless incorrect astrological forecasts in Tycho Brahe's time. Rudolf Steiner's criticism of astrology is therefore fully justified.

The decline of astrological knowledge on the one hand and humanity's turn to purely physical science since the Age of

Enlightenment have been accompanied by a radical change in the world view. But, today's modern world view is by no means the non-plus-ultra of knowledge. We should remember that it was only around 200 years ago that the idea of a purely materialistic universe gradually became established in the West, together with the denial of the existence of extrasensory beings.

Until 100 years ago, nothing was known about distant galaxies. Astronomers were convinced that our Milky Way was the only galaxy in the universe. It was not until 1923 that the American astronomer Edwin Hubble succeeded in proving that the Andromeda Nebula is located outside the Milky Way and is a galaxy of its own. This broke a new frontier of knowledge. Since then, researchers have discovered billions of other galaxies by means of ever more sensitive telescopes. With each new type of telescope, countless more are added. As a result, astronomers' estimates of the size of the universe change from decade to decade. Many of them now consider the Big Bang theory, which has become so popular, to be outdated.

Science will gradually overcome further boundaries and unbiased researchers will eventually no longer be able to deny the existence of higher levels of existence and beings. In this way, some natural scientists will eventually find their way to spiritual science. Just as Columbus once did not "discover" America, but "rediscovered" it after its existence had been lost to the consciousness of Europeans for several centuries, researchers of the future will also rediscover the extrasensory worlds and their inhabitants that had been suppressed from the consciousness of the Western world for several centuries. Then the fundamental unity of the ancient world view with the new world view will be recognized and the knowledge of ancient cultures will finally receive the appreciation it deserves.

List of Figures

Abb. 1:	The spheres of our solar system in Schedel's World Chronicle (1493)	27
Abb. 2:	Rudolf Steiner's sketch on the two-dimensional spatial areas of the zodiac	37
Abb. 3:	The spheres of our solar system in the Cosmographia of Peter Apian (1539 edition)	45
Abb. 4:	Table of corrections for the ephemeris from the year 1413 onwards	53
Abb. 5:	The gradual loss of knowledge of the zodiac	59
Abb. 6:	Synopsis of the ancient world view with today's world view	65
Abb. 7:	The two main axes of the year in the Age of Taurus	72
Abb. 8:	Rudolf Steiner's sketch on the effectiveness of the forces of the zodiac during the course of the day	79
Abb. 9:	The positions of Mercury on the evening of the laying of the foundation stone for the first Goetheanum, according to Rudolf Steiner's house system	88

Roland Schrapp

The Anthroposophical Soul Calendar and the Incarnation Cycle of Man

Publisher:
BoD – Books on Demand, Norderstedt (Germany)

Large format (DIN A4)
270 pages, 27 illustrations

Paperback (adhesive binding):
ISBN: 9783752690101

Hardcover (thread binding):
ISBN: 9783752602906

This book takes a completely new look at the Anthroposophical Soul Calendar. It is about the deeper meaning of the fifty-two weekly verses, which has remained essentially unexplored in the last hundred years since the first edition by Rudolf Steiner. A dense veil of Isis was spread over them, of which is well known that no mortal person can lift it. Only the immortal, psycho-spiritual human being, who knows himself at home in the extrasensory, higher worlds, is capable of doing this. Only to him the weekly verses reveal themselves as a travel guide through these worlds and lift him up to ever higher spiritual-cosmic realms until he reaches the experience of God, from where he gradually descends again into a new life on Earth, enriched in spirit and fertilized in his soul. If the reader embarks on this journey, the spiritual archetype of the Soul Calendar is ultimately unveiled to him and he achieves an extended understanding of Man and Christ. By many quotations from Rudolf Steiner's lectures and books, the author virtually lets Steiner himself elucidate the breathtaking depths of his mysterious weekly verses.

Roland Schrapp

Publisher:
BoD – Books on Demand,
Norderstedt (Germany)

Paperback:
178 pages, 18 illustrations

ISBN: 9783743124585

Between death and a new birth on earth, the human being lives through a long cosmic existence in the higher worlds. This is mirrored in the earthly life. Rudolf Steiner described its division into seven-year periods and the connection with the pre-birth existence in the planetary spheres. Apart from this, there is another division including higher spheres of the fixed stars. Rudolf Steiner only gave us a hint. In line whith this and based on his own experiences on the path of spirit discipleship, the author of this book gives examples how these different stages of life between death and rebirth can express themselves in the course of earthly life. He also explains in which of the seven-year periods the conditions for learning something about one's own previous incarnation are particularly favourable. In addition, he describes the connection of the later seven-year periods of earthly life with the Life Spirit (Budhi), as well as the preparation of mankind for receiving it by a development which Rudolf Steiner called the gradual "getting-younger" of mankind, and which started at the times of the primeval Semites in ancient Atlantis.

Roland Schrapp

Publisher:
BoD – Books on Demand
Norderstedt (Germany)

Paperback:
81 pages, 6 illustrations

ISBN: 9783755717072

This book is not a mere summary of Rudolf Steiner's statements on the connection of the forces of the zodiac with the ages, but it offers a whole new range of view points on astrology, astronomy and the cultural history of mankind. The author first describes the origin of the zodiacal images according to Rudolf Steiner's statements. Then he discusses why these images do not correspond either with the signs of the zodiac in traditional astrology or with the physically visible constellations of the stars, and what role the astronomy of the ancient Greeks plays in this. It is also explained why, when creating a horoscope, the planetary positions must not simply be taken over unchanged from the ephemerides. They need a correction due to the precession of the vernal equinox. This makes the book a "must have" for every astrologically interested person. Another topic is the varying duration of the ages and what questions this raises for modern astronomy. Finally, using the example of European cultural development over the last thousand years, it is shown that each age is divided into twelve smaller cultural periods, which in their characteristics correspond exactly to the series of the zodiacal forces. In this way it becomes understandable why the cultural development of mankind just happened the way it did.

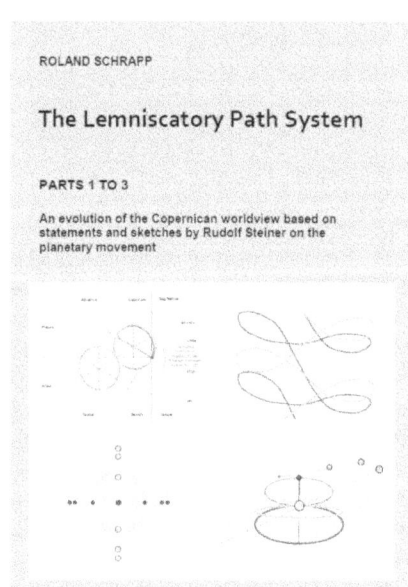

Roland Schrapp

Publisher:
BoD – Books on Demand, Norderstedt (Germany)

Paperback: 198 pages
Large format (DIN A4)
253 mostly coloured illustrations

ISBN: 9783752604030

An evolution of the Copernican worldview based on statements and sketches by Rudolf Steiner on the planetary movement.

For the first time in almost a hundred years, Rudolf Steiner's statements and sketches on the subject of the "lemniscatory paths of the planets", distributed over several lecture cycles, have been brought into a larger context and examined for the consequences of this. Steiner's suggestions for a new consideration of the planetary movement were taken up and tried to develop them further in the given sense. The work "The Lemniscatory Path System" arose from this. The treatise comprises 192 pages with 253 mostly coloured illustrations.

Milton Keynes UK
Ingram Content Group UK Ltd.
UKHW010150270624
444787UK00001B/40